Spreading HIS Fame

Kris Segrest, D.Min.

Pulpit Press
www.pulpit-press.com

Copyright © Kris Segrest, D.Min.
kris@churchforthecities.org

All Scripture is from the English Standard Version (ESV) unless otherwise noted. All emphasis has been added by the author.

The Holy Bible, English Standard Version® (ESV®)
Copyright © 2001 by Crossway,
a publishing ministry of Good News Publishers.
All rights reserved.
ESV Text Edition: 2011

Scriptures taken from the Holy Bible, New International Version®, NIV®. Copyright © 1973, 1978, 1984, 2011 by Biblica, Inc.™ Used by permission of Zondervan. All rights reserved worldwide. www.zondervan.com The "NIV" and "New International Version" are trademarks registered in the United States Patent and Trademark Office by Biblica, Inc.™

Contents

Introduction 1

It's Not about You 5

Holy Moments 17

Glory Chasers 29

Forsaking Glory 42

Faith Ratchets Up 59

There Is No Glory in the Expected 73

Grow Up as Fast as You Can 88

Superpowers 104

The Final Warning: The Scariest Story in the Bible 116

Endnotes 131

Acknowledgments

To Amy, the love of my life and friend.

To Rook and Molly, the two best gifts God has given me.

To the people of First Baptist Church Wylie, a people who "Spread HIS Fame."

Introduction

This is a book about glory. We don't talk much about glory. In fact, it is not a word we use often or much. My earliest remembrance of someone using the word was when my charismatic second cousin screamed, "Glorrrry!" at a family reunion. Most likely she really liked the baked beans.

The bottom line is God is all about glory, and we, Christ followers, don't really know that much about it. Or at least I was not aware of God's commitment to His glory. I grew up in a pragmatic church where if we do this, God will do that. It has taken me decades to unlearn this behavior of trying to perform so God would work for me.

As a pastor in the Dallas-Fort Worth metroplex, you can't drive to your church without passing five other churches on the way. A few years ago our faith family began to try to figure out what it means to follow Christ in the context of suburbia. We arrived at this purpose statement:

"Spreading God's fame, by making disciples of all people."

This content of this statement is dense enough for a person and a church to live their lives on. It is rooted in the vision of *spreading God's fame*. When we talk about spreading God's fame, we are talking about His glory. The best way for us to relate practically to God's glory is in respect to fame. We all know what being famous is about; it is being well known.

Every night on television, we see shows like *TMZ* and *Extra* that do nothing but chase famous people around documenting the most mundane detail. Celebrity culture has become insane. The fact that we even know who the Kardashians are is a testimony to our pursuit of trivial things.

The Bible says God demands to be made famous. His glory demands it. As a church and a people, we want to spread His fame in everything we do. Only that which is eternal is going to last. And only that which is eternal is worth our lives.

But having a vision of spreading His fame has a direct effect—a mission. We spread His fame *by making disciples*. Not only is disciple making prescribed and commanded by Jesus, but it is also the natural by-product of our affections and loyalties.

I live in Texas. People drive a lot of trucks in Texas. There are all kinds of different trucks to choose from, but two stand out—Ford and Chevrolet. I know one guy who is so loyal to Chevrolet that if you gave him a free Ford, he would give it back to you. He can tell you story after story about the greatness of Chevy. He has found a great product, and he endorses it wholeheartedly. He makes disciples for Chevy whenever the topic of automobiles finds its way into his conversations.

In the same way, when you and I realize the awesomeness of God, it flavors our words and deeds. We can't help but indoctrinate people in our path because we are so convinced about the greatness of our God.

And finally, having a vision and mission gives us a goal. We say it like this, "Spreading God's fame, by making disciples *of all people."* When you are convinced about how awesome God is and you understand the mission of disciple making, you realize that you must love the people God loves. Whom does God love? Everyone!

We take the glory of God to the toughest people, in the toughest places, with the toughest problems because only God can fix what is broken. This past year we sent a team to one of the most deadly countries in the world for Christians. I remember a man asking me, "Why would we send people to such a dangerous place?" My response, "Because God loves those people. And if we don't go, who will?"

This book is simply the first few steps on our journey, as a faith family and individuals, into the glory of God. I hope you are challenged and changed by what you read.

Chapter 1
It's Not about You

You may not want to read much of this book after you read the first few pages. I wouldn't blame you. These words might not sit well with many of you. If you go to church, you're more likely to be shocked and dumbfounded at what you are about to read. Here it is: the Bible, the world, heaven, Jesus, and God Himself are not about you. In fact, God is radically, passionately, completely centered on Himself. God is indescribably into Himself. Let that sink in for a moment. You are not the center of the universe.

This hit me many years ago after a series of disappointments with God. Yes, I said it. I was disappointed with how God was treating me. And then I began to read the Scriptures and realized the majority of the Bible was all about God, not me. I call this the Glory Principle. The Glory Principle states that "God works, first, for His glory and then my good." What is on the mind of God right now, all day, every day is how He will get glory out of all things.

How We Got Here

Now some of you reading this understand the reality that you are not the center of the universe and not everything is about you. But, before you give yourself that much credit, think about your life. How much of your life is organized and orchestrated largely around you, your people, your dreams, your desires, your schedule, your comfort, and your self-interest? If you really think about it, most of our lives are all about us. The natural default switch on the dial of our lives is us!

Our culture is more obsessed with itself today than ever before. We are the epitome of narcissists. In the last few generations, narcissism has risen to an all new high. The baby boomer generation, those born to the World War II generation, were largely all about themselves. They took prayer out of school. They gave us abortion so that immorality would no longer have consequences. They had more divorce than any generation before them. They lived up to their name—the Me Generation. The baby boomers wanted to cast off any restraint that hindered their individual freedom. It is all about me. (If this describes you, please know I like your generation. it is my parents' generation, and without my parents I would not be here. But you, just like every generation since, have really messed up some things in Western culture.)

The baby boomers produced the Xers, my generation, and we took narcissism to a whole new level. My generation created reality TV. The funny thing is, reality TV is void of any reality. The Xers so lowered the bar on fame that any immoral, irreverent, goofball could not only get his or her fifteen minutes of fame, but they could parlay it into a career. There is no way to estimate the radically damaging and damning effect this has had on culture. We collectively are dumber, having subjected ourselves to such narcissism. What draws us into the nonreality reality genre is thinking, in the back of our minds, *That could be me.* It is all about me.

Which brings us to the millennials, those persons born between 1980 and 2000. They are unequivocally the most narcissistic generation ever produced on human record. With the advent of Facebook, Twitter, and an ever-growing number of social media outlets, we now have the capability to keep up-to-date on every trivial detail and even those we would rather not know from millennials, who are quickly becoming known as the iGeneration. Frankly, who cares where you have "checked in," how many pretend "friends" you have, and what you "like"? Only people who are enamored with themselves would. While social media definitely has some positives when handled improperly, it becomes a new scoreboard, which breeds self-obsession and discontent.

At least with this last group, the millennials, you can understand their narcissist tendencies. I mean, they have been raised by a generation that has turned them into demigods. The parents of the millennials—my generation, the Xers—were trying to make up for the deficiencies they perceived they received from their parents. So millennials have never been told no. They all can be straight-A students, be the head cheerleader or starting quarterback, and attend Ivy League schools. Further, if you are not good at any conventional activity, we will just make something up for you. This is the generation where everyone gets a trophy and a pat on the head. And you know what it has produced? A generation that lives longer on the dependency of their parents than any other generation before them. And the irony is, people are afraid to tell them to get off the couch. You see, when the world revolves around you and you suddenly realize you are not a god, it really affects your confidence and self-esteem.

Churches have, in many cases, not addressed this growing and present problem. In fact, they have helped propagate the issue. Preachers deliver message series that are focused on the felt needs of the people or the troubles of life or how to become prosperous. Complete with excellent facilities, state-of-the-art age-group areas, slick production, and free coffee, the lifestyles of the self-absorbed and narcissistic can be blessed and unchallenged in a timely manner.

Instead of taking people to the person of God and letting them gaze into His glory, we have, for fear of losing our crowds, created a generation of codependent narcissists who really are more concerned about where they will eat lunch and take their next vacation than they are about knowing personally and intimately a totally self-absorbed God.

Wow! you might be thinking, *This guy really has a problem with free coffee.* Actually, I am not against coffee; I love the glorious bean. But I guess I am really angry that no one, especially in the church, let me know earlier in life that the world does not revolve around me. It is not about me. It is all about Him. The goal of everything and everyone is God's glory, and that end results in His glory and then my good. God is not primarily concerned about improving my life, giving me a healthy self-esteem, and making me comfortable. He is about how His own glory or fame will spread in my life and to all people. He is obsessed with Himself and His own fame.

What scares me as a pastor is that the Bible clearly indicates that, "For the time is coming when people will not endure sound teaching, but having itching ears they will accumulate for themselves teachers to suit their own passions" (2 Tim. 4:3). I don't want to be guilty of being one of these teachers, leading lambs to slaughter. It makes sense that narcissistic crowds will clamor to hear pastors who will simply make the church and all of life about their selfish ends. In fact, I imagine these pastors will be well liked and well compensated, posers who have prostituted a religious system for their own gain. Now you might think I am being critical of others with these statements. You would be wrong. I am including myself here. I have been a part of a dynamically growing church over the past few years. So I am not down on growth in churches. In fact, I believe it can be used to measure the health of the church. But we must be careful what we preach and how we lead. It is entirely possible to grow a Christian-ish organization that worships at the altar of self and is blessed by a guy who went to seminary. This concerns me. We can be into church, or community, or a communicator, or ministry and missions and not be into this absolutely self-absorbed God, who is obsessed with His own glory.

God loves Himself more than anything or anyone. Think about it like this: God has no other choice but to be self-centered. Who or what is greater than God in all the universe? No one. Nothing. When you are God, the only person you can dwell on is Yourself. When people think of themselves in this way, we become idolaters because we are not the greatest person or thing in the universe, but God has no other alternative. If He does not relate to Himself in this way, He becomes an idolater; He worships something or someone lesser than Himself. Therefore, contrary to popular belief, God's highest thoughts are not you or me but Himself. His narcissism has been and continues to be what motivates Him.

God Is All about Himself

Here is the deal: the Bible is not a story about me or you. Let that sink in a minute. Many of us grew up on a steady diet of why the Bible was about me—my fallen state, my salvation through Christ, my ultimately going to heaven. First and foremost, the Bible is a story about how God is going to get His glory—this is His motivation and ultimate end. God is doing all things for His own fame. It has always been this way. We may have not picked it up, but it has always been there. People are fine with a God demanding our attention as long as we can demand His attention. John Piper says: "Many people are willing to be god-centered as long as they feel that God is man-centered. It is a subtle danger. We may think that we are centering our lives on God, when we are really making Him a means to self-esteem."[1] Did you catch that? We might not be motivated by what God is, His fame, but our own self-esteem. We really want a God who will take care of us, keep us pain-free and blessed. But God is passionately more concerned about His own interests, mainly His glory. He says in Isaiah 42:8, "I am the Lord; that is my name; my glory I give to no other, nor my praise to carved idols." God will not relent in His passion and primacy of Himself. The Bible, from beginning to end, Genesis to maps, is a story of His glory—His fame.

All of creation testifies to His glory, according to the Bible. "Worthy are you, our Lord and God, to receive *glory* and honor and power, for you created all things, and by your will they existed and were created" (Rev. 4:11). There are no accidents. Whether a muskrat or a mountain, God made them both, and each one extols His awesome creativity in creation. The psalmist says, "Be exalted, O God, above the heavens! Let your *glory* be over all the earth!" (Ps. 108:5). When we look into the sky, we see the handiwork of God in the nighttime sky. He even goes so far as to name each one of the stars, "Lift up your eyes on high and see: who created these? He who brings out their host by number, calling them all by name, by the *greatness of his might*, and because *he is strong in power* not one is missing" (Isa. 40:26). And He does all this, without even breaking a sweat, every night. The oceans remind us of his limitless fame, "For the earth will be filled with the *knowledge of the glory of the Lord* as the waters cover the sea" (Hab. 2:14).

And to top off the creation, He created man for His own glory. Genesis 1:27 says, "So God created man in his own image, in the image of God he created him; male and female he created them." Man was given this special status in creation. We humans are made in the *Imago Dei* or the image of God. We are not God, but we are a reflection of the reality of who He is. What man is in part, God is in whole. It gets even better: according to Scripture, "Bring my sons from afar and my daughters from the end of the earth, everyone who is called by my name, whom I created for *my glory*" (Isa. 43:6–7). God is determined to get glory out of you and me.

Scripture testifies that the salvation of people and nations is for His glory. This is why He defeated Pharaoh in Egypt on behalf of Israel. "And I will harden Pharaoh's heart, and he will pursue them, and I will get glory over Pharaoh and all his host, and the Egyptians shall know that I am the Lord" (Exod. 14:4). His fame is why He even brought Israel out of Egypt, "Our fathers, when they were in Egypt, did not consider your wondrous works . . . but rebelled by the sea, at the Red Sea. *Yet he saved them for his name's sake, that he might make known his mighty power*" (Ps. 106:7–8). Despite Israel's continued obstinacy and rebellion, He continued to save them for His own fame, "I *acted for the sake of my name*, that it should not be profaned in the sight of the nations, in whose sight I had brought them out" (Ezek. 20:14).

And most personally, the Bible says, God saves you and me for His glory. Ephesians 1:11–12: "In him we have obtained an inheritance, having been predestined according to the purpose of him who works all things according to the counsel of his will, so that we who were the first to hope in Christ might be to the *praise of his glory*." You and I were saved primarily for His own boasting, not for any other reason. I was taught that the reason I was saved was to get out of hell. I hate to be that blunt, but I suspect that was the primary motivation of many people who trusted in Christ was to get out of hell. I mean, hell has never worked out for anyone, and I can appreciate not wanting to rot there for eternity, but escaping hell is not the primary reason for salvation—it is God's glory. He saves you to get glory from you: "In the same way, let your light shine before others, so that they may see your good works and *give glory* to your Father who is in heaven" (Matt. 5:16).

His laws demand that He receives His glory. The first two laws of the Ten Commandments deal directly with the fame of God in the lives of His people, "You shall have no other gods before me. "You shall not make for yourself a carved image, or any likeness of anything that is in heaven above, or that is in the earth beneath, or that is in the water under the earth. You shall not bow down to them or serve them, for I the Lord your God am a jealous God, visiting the iniquity of the fathers on the children to the third and the fourth generation of those who hate me, but showing steadfast love to thousands of those who love me and keep my commandments" (Exod. 20:3–6). God demands that His fame be the most important priority for His people, and He will not to be misrepresented in any way.

God's name literally brings Him glory. Psalm 96:8 says, "Ascribe to the Lord the glory due his name; bring an offering, and come into his courts!" Psalm 115:1 reiterates this claim, "Not to us, O Lord, not to us, but to your name give glory, for the sake of your steadfast love and your faithfulness!" God's name is not to be profaned or desecrated. It is not to be used casually or without regard. So the next time you hear a curse word, let it grieve your Spirit because it does not give God glory, and don't be afraid to correct such defamatory talk. God's name is attached to His person,

His character, His glory. When you hear His name, you ought to think about Him. When people mention your name, something immediately comes to their mind. In the same way God's name ought to trigger proper thoughts about Him.

The Scripture helps us see that Jesus was primarily sent to give God glory. All Jesus' work was for God's glory. "The one who speaks on his own authority seeks his own glory; but the one who seeks the *glory of him who sent him is true*, and in him there is no falsehood" (John 7:18). Jesus endured hardship and suffering for the Father's glory, "'Now is my soul troubled. And what shall I say? "Father, save me from this hour"? But for this purpose I have come to this hour. Father, glorify your name.' Then a voice came from heaven, '*I have glorified it, and I will glorify it again*'" (John 12:27–28). Christ's death and resurrection bring God glory, "And being found in human form, he humbled himself by becoming obedient to the point of death, even death on a cross. Therefore God has highly exalted him and bestowed on him the name that is above every name, so that at the name of Jesus every knee should bow, in heaven and on earth and under the earth, and every tongue confess that Jesus Christ is Lord, to the *glory of God the Father*" (Phil. 2:8–11).

This is a radically different slant on the gospel than I grew up being told. I was taught that Jesus came to save me. It was all about me. I never heard about God getting His glory out of these events. It is harsh to say but true—I was convinced growing up that I was doing God a favor joining His team. A number of years ago, my son was invited to another kid's birthday party. Admittedly this boy was not the most popular of all the kids at school, but we were trying to teach our son to be friends with everyone. When my wife dropped him off, my son was the only one that attended the party. My wife was relieved that someone had come to this poor child's birthday party. She's the compassionate one in our family and arguably the real Christian. Needless to say, he had a great goodie bag that day, but I digress. Imagine the emotional and mental damage that could have been done to this child if no one had come to his party? I have heard some appeals to would-be followers that portray God in this manner, like a kid who can't get anyone to come to his party. This is a completely false understanding of God. God is completely self-sufficient in Himself. It wasn't like He got bored in heaven one day and created us to have some little playmates. No, God did all this and more so He could get glory, fame, renown.

The Bible tells us that the means for all ministry is intended to get God greater glory. Prayer is a tool by which God gets glory, "Whatever you ask in my name, this I will do, *that the Father may be glorified* in the Son" (John 14:13). The Holy Spirit in our lives gives glory to God. "He [the Holy Spirit] *will glorify* me, for he will take what is mine and declare it to you " (John 16:14). Our service points to God's glory, "Whoever serves, [let him do it] as one who serves by the strength which God supplies—*in order that in everything God may be glorified* through Jesus Christ. To him belong glory and dominion forever and ever. Amen" (1 Pet. 4:11).

Scripture affirms that the consummation of the age, meaning the return of Christ, will be intended to bring God His glory. The wrath of God upon those who have rejected Him will make Him more glorious, "Desiring to show his wrath and to make known his power, [God] has endured with much patience vessels of wrath prepared for destruction, *in order to make known the riches of his glory for vessels of mercy*, which he prepared beforehand for glory" (Rom. 9:22–23). What the most vile, godless people on the earth do not know is that even their rebellion will reveal God's glory.

Further, "they will suffer the punishment of eternal destruction, away from the presence of the Lord and *from the glory of his might, when he comes on that day to be glorified in his saints*, and to be marveled at among all who have believed" (2 Thess. 1:9–10). You see, the good news is that He makes a way of salvation for us but mainly for His glory. And when you have experienced this undeserved salvation, it makes Him look even more glorious.

And if all this discourse in the Scripture about glory was not enough, God's own glory will light up eternity. In the New Jerusalem, "the city has no need of sun or moon to shine on it, *for the glory of God gives it light*, and its lamp is the Lamb" (Rev. 21:23). Think about it: the person and power of God's glory will light up all of eternity. It will make the sun look dim.

Now all of this talk of God's infinite glory is a lot to take in. Yes? And you might be wondering, *How do I fit into all of this?* How does being a student, a parent, a business owner, an employee, a missionary, or a minister work in light of God's glory. Well, let me assure you that there is a place for you in all of this. God works first and foremost for His own glory but then for our good. For right now wrestle with the reality that God is more centered on Himself than He is about you; and that, believe it or not, is a really good thing—as you will see.

Questions

1. How is God getting glory from you right now? In what part of your life?

2. Where in the world is God getting glory?

3. Where does God need to get glory from you? In what part of the world? What will you do about that?

Chapter 2
Holy Moments

Some moments completely redefine every other moment after that. As the Lord deals with us, divine moments have eternal ramifications for our lives. I remember, distinctly, as a nine-year-old boy, trusting Christ as my Savior and Lord. We lived in Bossier City, Louisiana, where my dad worked in the oil field and my mom was a homemaker. We had attended church on and off until the crash of the United States economy beginning in the 1980s. After that we were back in church. It really is amazing how when things are good we typically don't need God, but when things go bad, we're quick to run back to Him. I'm glad things worked out the way they did because I might not have known who Jesus is.

So, on a Thursday night as a nine-year-old boy, after asking many questions about Jesus, I bent a knee, knelt on a piano bench in the living room of our house with our pastor and my parents, and I asked Christ to come into my life. I didn't really know exactly what I had done, but I knew it was life changing. I mean, there was no burning bush or pillar of fire, but I knew this was a significant moment, and it would change all the moments to come. This was my first *holy moment*. Over the next few years, I attended church and did all the things a little Christian kid does. However, deep within me I knew there was something more to this than simply going to a church building, dropping my dollar in the plate, and singing songs while sitting on uncomfortable furniture.

We moved from Louisiana back to North Texas, where I have remained most of my life. I moved to my mother's hometown, and it quickly became my own. We began to attend another church, and, as a sixth-grader, I went to summer camp. At that summer camp I had my second *holy moment*. I began to realize that I had done more by asking Christ into my life than simply saying a prayer. I immediately began to question if I really knew what I was doing as a nine-year-old kid. See, when you're a little kid, you have no idea about the depravity of the world. You probably haven't knocked over too many liquor stores, cheated on your taxes, or plunged yourself into debased immorality. But as a teenager you start understanding what sin really is. You can conceptualize the reality between your personal sins and Christ's death on the cross—not just for the world but for you. You begin to realize, while you have not acted out many outrageous sins, the potential is in you.

So I began to question if I really knew what I had done. Did I really know Jesus, or did I go through some religious rite of passage. A friend named Lynn, an older believer used by God, helped me in this *holy moment*. He shared with me the great truth found in Ephesians 2:8, "For by grace you have been saved through faith. And this is not your own doing; it is the gift of God." He went on to explain that you could not lose what you had never earned. He compared a relationship with Jesus Christ to a train. The engine is essential to make a train move. The boxcars, behind the engine, can be manipulated in any order. Lynn went on to say that faith is essential to saving grace; it's like the engine. Our feelings, which vary from day to day and hour by hour, are like the boxcars. While feelings are important, they're not essential to faith.

In that moment I first understood intimacy with Jesus. I was overwhelmed with His great love for me and moved by

His goodness. Understanding how much I was loved, I began to immerse myself in the Bible. I didn't really know what I was doing; I just started reading. I found this old Living Bible in the house. Every single verse just seemed to the leap off the page. To ensure I would not forget where verses were found, I began to create my own tabs. They were makeshift pieces of paper and scotch tape. I used made-up hieroglyphics only to be understood by me. I was captivated by Jesus. Biblical Christianity is a relationship, not a religion.

One of the essentials to growing in faith with Jesus is simply to fall in love with Him. Affection will take you much further and deeper than discipline ever will. Now don't get me wrong—there is a place for discipline in the Christian life. That's why Christ followers are called disciples. But, when you genuinely love someone, there is nothing you will not do to please, protect, and persevere in that relationship. I have found that men, specifically, have a hard time relating to Jesus in a love relationship. Men in our day seem to have been robbed of genuine masculinity, which includes love. When you think about masculinity, you have to think about Jesus. Jesus was a burly carpenter who spent time around fisherman, ruffians, and other ne'er-do-wells. No one ever challenged the masculinity of Jesus. Yet Jesus is the essence of love. Love is not always giving someone what they want but what they need. This is exactly how Jesus loved. If men are ever going to grow in their relationship with God, they will have to get over this cultural perversity of masculinity and begin to understand what it means to love like Jesus. Jesus used His power to serve others.

A few years later I had another moment, a *holy moment*. I was in my teenage years and thought I had a life plan figured out. I was completely convinced that I would one day become an attorney. Now I don't mean the ambulance-chasing, duplicitous, money-sucking lawyers you see on TV and billboards. I was going to be one of the good guys. One of those attorneys who sticks up for the little guy and the underdog. I felt I was uniquely equipped for such a career path. After all, I really like to argue. I like to see justice served, and all of the lawyers I knew had nice, comfortable lifestyles—that was a winning combination. While I never experienced much want, money had always been an issue in my home growing up. I thought this would be the answer to all of my concerns. I could follow Jesus and be comfortable. Sometimes you really don't want Jesus to mess up your plan, and that's about the time He does.

Once again I was at a camp, and all week long I began to feel God calling me into full-time ministry. Now, before you think this doesn't apply to you, I want to remind you that every person who is a Christ follower is called to serve Him with their life, all of their life. For some of you, that may be in the marketplace; for others that may be in the home. For some that may be in education; for some that may be in civic office. But everyone is called to full-time ministry. More and more I see God calling people out of various sectors of culture and using them in full-time ministry. Never say, "Never!" I promise that is always a bad plan. Christ has the authority and right to reorganize your life however He wants to.

I believe people experience two kinds of callings in life as it pertains to ministry. There's a calling like my friend Dennis, who has just said yes when opportunities presented themselves, and God keeps sending him more opportunities. I would compare him to the early disciples who first spent a day with Jesus, then dropped their nets for a short season with Jesus, and then dropped their nets permanently to follow Jesus. This might be how it plays out for you.

For me, however, I experienced more of a clarion call. I knew God was calling me into ministry and that I had no choice in the matter. I will simply tell you this: I did not go easy. While I love Jesus, there were some other things I really wanted to do. My calling was more like Paul on the Damascus Road. Like Paul, I was surrounded by witnesses—in my case a few hundred pubescent teenagers, who smelled like feet and Doritos. But for me a light shone out of heaven that has forever changed the trajectory of my life to this very moment. It became glaringly apparent to me that I would never be fulfilled until I completely yielded my life to His will. For me these experiences were the beginning, of many Isaiah 6 *holy moments*.

Isaiah 6 is one of the most foundational Scriptures in all my life. No other Scripture so eloquently outlines the essentials of a holy moment. Isaiah, the prophet, makes his way into the temple in Jerusalem to pay respects to a dead king named Uzziah, who had, for the most part, been a good king for the people of Israel. If you've ever been to a funeral, you could relate. As a pastor I spend a more than average amount of time in funeral homes. Funerals in general are interesting. Depending on the faith of the deceased and the family members that survive, there is no telling what you'll find. I have found, for people who know Jesus and their families, funerals are generally affirming and a celebration of what God did in the life of the believer. However, for people who don't know Jesus or their family members who don't know Jesus, funerals can become a dog and pony show. In fact, my experience, the more uncertain a person's eternal security is, the longer the funeral goes (I'm just saying). Israel always struggled to find godly leaders, and Uzziah had led them well, but now the people and Isaiah are trying to figure out what life will look like from this day forward.

As Isaiah enters the temple, to his surprise he does not pay homage to a dead king. He encounters the eternal, living King of the universe—God. Notice what Isaiah 6:1–5 says:

> In the year that King Uzziah died, I saw the Lord sitting upon a throne, high and lifted up; and the train of his robe filled the temple. Above him stood the seraphim. Each had six wings: with two he covered his face, and with two he covered his feet, and with two he flew. And one called to another and said:
>
> "Holy, holy, holy is the Lord of hosts; the whole earth is full of his glory!"
>
> And the foundations of the thresholds shook at the voice of him who called, and the house was filled with smoke. And I said: "Woe is me! For I am lost; for I am a man of unclean lips, and I dwell in the midst of a people of unclean lips; for my eyes have seen the King, the Lord of hosts!"

Isaiah finds himself enveloped in a *holy moment*, a moment that will radically and permanently affect all the other moments of his life. One of the first details of this story that alters Isaiah's reality forever is the awesomeness of God. *Awesome* is a word that has become wasted on lesser things. *Awesome* has been used to describe everything from food, people, experiences, you name it. *Awesome* has an interesting definition because it means "impressive or daunting"; It can mean "inspiring or dreadful or formidable." It is a disturbing word when you really think about it. It essentially means "terrifically terrifying." So only one being can accurately be described as awesome, solely and only—God.

Isaiah had a one-on-one moment with a holy God who was terrifically terrifying in the totality of who He is. What makes God so distinctively different, so awesome? It is His holiness. The seraphim, or angels, hovering around the throne of God, exclaiming that He was not just holy but *holy, holy, holy*. We don't really understand holiness, but let me try to demonstrate. God's holiness is the be-all from which all other attributes flow. It is what makes Him God. God does not just love; He has a holy love. God is not just merciful; He is holy in his mercy. *Holiness* means "to be set apart." God's holiness makes Him completely different and completely set apart from anyone or anything else in all of creation. It makes Him awesome.

Isaiah sees this holy God, and he is blown away by God's awesomeness. Has this ever happened to you? When a person has this kind of encounter with God, it is called a theophany. Peter and his companions in the New Testament, after they catch an outrageous number of fish, recognize who Jesus really is—God. These men, like Isaiah, were changed in a moment when they realized who God was. Have you ever seen God just for who He is?

In many ways we, as believers, have minimalized our awesome God. Many Christians today handle God casually. To combat the legalism of former generations, many believers in the modern church have allowed the pendulum to swing to the other extreme—an extreme that makes God in my own image. Jesus is my "buddy," and God is a benevolent grandfather who wants me to be happy. We need to remember that God is not like us. In His goodness He sent Christ to identify with us, but the essence of God is not me or you. We must recapture a sense of the holy.

But God's awesomeness is not just to be admired like Christmas lights on a gaudy holiday house. Seeing Him has a radical effect on people. The text says that "the foundations of the thresholds shook . . . and the house was filled with smoke." There's a word we don't use much, and it's the word *glory*. God's awesome attribute of holiness manifests itself in the weight of His glory. Glory is the physical manifestation of God's holiness on the earth. God is all about the display of His glory in the world and in our lives. His glory gets on you—like smoke.

Have you ever been around a person who smokes? No matter how hard they try to mask it, everyone can tell. When I was a student minister, there was this kid who was a chain-smoker. I don't know how you can be as young as he was and be a chain-smoker, but I guess practice makes perfect. Anyway, this kid would always go outside the church, sneak off the property, and smoke. He would come back into the building with a Tic Tac in his mouth, thinking that one little mint would mask his smoky aroma. We could tell he had been smoking. And by the way, if you smoke, people know—they can smell it on you. I digress. When a person has been in the presence of God, people can tell. The "smoke" of God stays on them. What do you smell like?

Seeing God for who He is, in all of His glory, brings about a conviction as to who we are. Isaiah, the prophet, immediately realizes he is a sin-stained man. For he says, "Woe is me!" The word *woe* is not a word we use often, if at all, but this word *woe* means "to be blown apart at the seams." It is like a man who squats down and rips apart the seam of his pants. While it might be funny watching someone split his pants, and it is, Isaiah was not laughing at this moment. He is undone. He is embarrassed. He cannot hide. And this is the state that Isaiah finds himself—and all people find themselves—in when they have been confronted with who God is in light of who they are. When you recognize who God is in light of who you are, you are blown apart at the seams. You don't make excuses. You don't justify your actions or lifestyle. You don't make deals. You simply fall down because of the weight of His holiness and glory. That is exactly what Isaiah does and what we do.

When you meet God in this manner, it is like looking into the sun and having to turn away because you become blinded. Unlike the Christian self-help section of the local bookstore, when sinful people meet this holy God, they are wrecked, and their world is blown apart. Have you ever been wrecked? Has your world ever been turned upside down in light of meeting this holy God? If not, that might be the problem.

The text goes on to say in Isaiah 6:6–7: "Then one of the seraphim flew to me, having in his hand a burning coal that he had taken with tongs from the altar. And he touched my mouth and said: 'Behold, this has touched your lips; your guilt is taken away, and your sin atoned for.'"

Do you really like justice? Many people think they really want to see justice prevail until they are the one about to receive it. On April 15, 2013, the Boston Marathon was interrupted by a series of terrorist bomb blasts. What was supposed to be a day of celebration quickly became a day of tragedy. In the hours that followed, it became apparent that two Chechen brothers were responsible for the attack, which led to the deaths of three individuals and injured hundreds in the explosions. Dzhokhar and Tamerlan Tsarnaev, two brothers, became infamous overnight. The eldest, Dzhokhar, was killed by police in a gun battle. The younger, Tamerlan, was later found wounded and hiding in a boat in a driveway. I vividly remember watching on TV the procession of emergency vehicles—police cars, fire trucks, National Guard vehicles, and the ambulance that took Tamerlan to the hospital. The streets of Boston were filled with angry men and women who wanted justice. As camera crews showed the faces of the people, patriotic chants, affirming the greatness of America, and profane curses, toward a would-be killer, both filled the air. As I sat back and watched these events unfold, I had to ask myself, *Do we all really want justice in our own lives with regard to an awesome God?* I mean, Do we really want a Holy God to give us what we deserve? I don't think so.

  I am so grateful God is not like us. He is awesome. When the weight of His glory brings about the wrecking of an individual, He is merciful in not giving us what we deserve. Notice the text details that an angel takes a burning coal to touch the sinful mouth of Isaiah. By doing so, the angel cleanses Isaiah's mouth so God can use him. Think about it: Isaiah's mouth is cauterized by burning coal so he can be used by God. Imagine taking a charcoal briquette that is lit, white hot, and placing it on your lips. I cannot imagine how painful that must've been. But I do know, in our holy moments, this is how an awesome God deals with us. It will be painful but productive.

  I do not like pain, especially mouth pain. A few years ago I got to experience the torture of what is known as a root canal. It was the most painful experience of my entire life. I don't believe in hitting women, but this lady was making me rethink my position. She put me through pain like I had never experienced before. She offered me gas, like I might refuse it. I said, "Turn it up till I see Jimi Hendrix." Then, to add insult to injury, she put on the movie for me to watch called *The Bucket List*, which is about two old men getting ready to die. It was like, *Is this doctor giving me a glimpse of my immediate future?* I have never hurt like that before or since. Eventually my pain went away. Pain can be productive, but no pain is bearable unless you understand the process. I knew the way to my ultimate healing was through this momentary pain—the dentist chair.

Notice how this holy moment ends for Isaiah. Verses 8–9 say: "And I heard the voice of the Lord saying, 'Whom shall I send, and who will go for us?' Then I said, 'Here am I! Send me.' And he said, 'Go.'"

Through this painful process Isaiah is now ready to be used by God. Notice, Isaiah does not hear God's voice until he has been made clean. In fact, one would gather that God doesn't even speak specifically to people who have not yet been purified. Or, perhaps, people who are caught up in the throes of sin simply can't hear God. At least in my life, every moment that has resulted in greater intimacy and experience with this awesome God has resulted in a prior process of painful purification. We have a tendency to tolerate sin and to lessen the profane, but God does not use dirty vessels to do His work, and He never relaxes His holy standards. If you're going to be used by him, you will most likely feel bruised by Him in advance.

I had a friend I grew up with. We spent nearly every day of our childhood together. We would ride bikes, without helmets—I know, crazy! We would eat snacks that included peanuts—I know, reckless! We would shoot BB guns at turtles—I know, barbaric! Here's the kicker—we made it to adulthood. Anyway, after a long afternoon of terrorizing the neighborhood, we would often get thirsty and need a drink. I would do all I could to plan our water break at my house. You know why? Because at his house the cups were always dirty. I don't know how they washed their dishes, but it didn't work. One time he got me a glass of water with bits of dried oatmeal floating in it.

No one likes to use a dirty cup. Neither does God. Before He can use us, He must clean us. Notice, He does the cleaning—not you. We can't self-impose a cleaning process on ourselves. Once we have been prepared, He will use us in His service. The good thing is this process can begin now. Isaiah's *holy moment* happened quickly. When he left God's presence, he was purified, but perfection was going to be a process—the process of a lifetime.

God is determined to get glory from your life. To experience all of Him will require all of you. There will be moments, holy moments, where His conviction will lead to cleansing. Cleansing will lead to you commissioning. The commissioning is where it is at! You will see it works for His glory and your good.

Questions

1. Where was Isaiah when his holy moment occurred? Is there any correlation to space and divine presence?

2. Have you ever had a moment, a holy moment, which now defines every other moment?

3. What sin do you need to get rid of? Are you willing to submit to whatever painful process may be required to be used by God?

Chapter 3
Glory Chasers

How does it affect you, knowing that God is radically committed to His own glory and fame? Realizing that God is in it for Himself, consumed by His own agenda, completely mesmerized by His own reputation, what is the implication for you? I mean, what choice do you really have? What are your options?

Believe it or not, God being centered on Himself is just exactly what you need. You see, God works for His glory and your good. Did you hear that? He works for your good. How can this be? How can God's narcissism be for your good? It is simple: He is the only one capable of meeting all of your needs and addressing all of your issues. He is omniscient, meaning He knows everything, including everything about you. Before a word is even on your tongue, God already knows it (Ps. 139:4). He is omnipotent, meaning He is all powerful, including the ability to reign over the minute details of your life. You are not to worry about your life. If God sustains the birds of the air, He has the ability to take care of you (Matt. 6:25–34). He is omnipresent, meaning He is everywhere at all times. For the believer He is always there. If we go to heaven or the depths of the sea, He is always with us (Ps. 139).

Don't you realize, God is the only one capable of satisfying the deep longings of your heart? No amount of money, pleasure, achievement, power, status, or human relationships can fill the void in you that only God can fill. Blaise Pascal, the French physicist, a

Christian, who actually penned more words of theology than he did science, said this, "There is a God-shaped vacuum in the heart of every man which cannot be filled by any created thing, but only by God, the Creator, made known through Jesus." It is good for us to be glory chasers, people who can't get enough of His blazing glory. This is why the Bible instructs us to do even the mundane things to His glory because His glory turns the mundane into the majestic. First Corinthians 10:31 says, "So, whether you eat or drink, or whatever you do, do all to the glory of God."

Glory Chasers

Anything in your life not connected to the glory of God is a waste of your time and will not matter in eternity—you are just chasing what doesn't matter. God has made things simple for us: we are to chase His glory in all that we do. He knows we are people who have a tendency to wander, people who are forgetful, people who can make trivial things into important things. Therefore, He makes it simple—"Live for My glory." God knows we will either chase His glory or our own. Either way we will chase glory. Are you the right kind of glory chaser? Because you are chasing something.

Knowing that God lives for His own glory, doesn't it make sense that if we live for His glory, we might be less frustrated in our own lives? If you are as concerned about His glory as He is, don't you think some things might happen in your life that would be inexplicable? Maybe you would get that promotion—not because it will help you, but it would promote God's glory. Think about it: if we were adamant about God's getting His due in our homes, don't you think it might help us know what things to say yes to and the things to say no to? Maybe outside entities would have less control over our homes. Don't you think God's glory would be helpful in making financial decisions? Maybe then, instead of figuring out what new luxury item we might buy for ourselves, we might be militant about how extra money might give God greater glory. I wouldn't be surprised then if God would choose to bless us with more finances so He could get greater glory from you. Don't you think God's glory could be incredibly instrumental for our good in determining whom our closest and best relationships ought to be with? Don't you think the state of marriages, many ending in divorce, is largely a product of people seeking their own happiness and not God's glory? It seems that an unquenchable obsession for God's glory is absolutely beneficial to our good.

Glory chasers know that only God's glory satisfies; everything else leaves us in want. Augustine said it like this, "Our hearts are restless until they find their rest in You." Perhaps that relentless gnawing in our gut, that keeps you up at night, finds you unfilled in the morning, and nags you all day is the need to become a glory chaser to the God-obsessed God. This has been true for glory chasers since the beginning.

Consider God's glory chaser Moses. Are you like Moses? Moses saw God do some incredible thing. We find his story in Exodus 33:13–20:

> "Now therefore, if I have found favor in your sight, please show me now your ways, that I may know you in order to find favor in your sight. Consider too that this nation is your people." And he said, "My presence will go with you, and I will give you rest." And he said to him, "If your presence will not go with me, do not bring us up from here. For how shall it be known that I have found favor in your sight, I and your people? Is it not in your going with us, so that we are distinct, I and your people, from every other people on the face of the earth?"

And the Lord said to Moses, "This very thing that you have spoken I will do, for you have found favor in my sight, and I know you by name." Moses said, "*Please show me your glory.*" And he said, "I will make all my goodness pass before you and will proclaim before you my name 'The Lord.' And I will be gracious to whom I will be gracious, and will show mercy on whom I will show mercy. But," he said, "you cannot see my face, for man shall not see me and live."

What is fascinating about this conversation between Moses and God is the background of their relationship. Moses had already experienced so much with God. He had already seen God do many incomprehensible things. I would dare say, any one experience Moses had with God would have been significant for a lifetime. Remember, Moses is called by God in the middle of the wilderness by a bush that was on fire but not being consumed by the flames (Exod. 3). Miracle!

God then gives Moses various proofs that He will use him in Egypt to free His people, the Israelites—including a staff that turned into a snake (Exod. 4). Mind-blowing! Moses sees God do ten incredible plagues in Egypt, ultimately freeing the people from the hand of Pharaoh. He sees miracles like blood in the Nile River and the Passover, where a death angel killed the firstborn of all people who did not have the blood of lamb smeared on their doorposts (Exod. 7–12). Unbelievable!

Then, after being pursued by the Egyptian army, because Pharaoh reneged on his agreement to let the Israelites go free, Moses sees the Red Sea part to form dry land. He leads the nation across the dry land only to turn and see the walls of water collapse and destroy the greatest army in the known world (Exod. 13–14; 15–17). Dumbfounding! But it gets better. God provides water for the people in the desert and gives them manna from heaven every day to meet their physical needs. Fascinating! Then on Mount Sinai

God establishes a formal covenant with Moses and the Israelites, making them His own people, a promise that was given to Abraham hundreds of years before and was coming into existence (Exod. 18–32).

Now let all of that sink in for a minute. If anyone had seen God do some incredible things, Moses was the man. And remember this, all Moses had seen God do to this point was for God's own glory. Yet Moses understood that God's glory was for his personal good. How do we know this? Because, when given a chance to request anything from God, Moses wants to see God's glory. Why? Because God's glory is the ultimate good for Moses.

Our Good and God's Glory

God's glory is for our good, as Moses knew, because God revealing His glory is an incredibly intimate experience; it is a personal presence. Moses had seen God move corporately among the people, but Moses wanted God to show him something privately—"Show me your glory." You will never live for God's glory publicly until you are convinced of it privately. Our public life is an overflow out of our private revelation. Glory chasers are consumed with the person of God. They are not simply content with public demonstration of God's glory; they need personal connection. These people burn with a white-hot passion to know God, not know about Him. They will not rest until they have God Himself. If this is to happen, God must reveal to you new facets of His character. Only God can do this by the way. God revealed Himself first to Moses at the burning bush, and God is now going to reveal more of Himself to Moses. If eternity will be about exploring all the wondrous depths of the character of God, how much more do we need revelation of

God's nature and character here and now. Moses was a man God trusted enough to show His glory to him.

Here is a tough question we must ask ourselves, "How much of God's person does He trust me with?" Early in Jesus' ministry He goes to Jerusalem where He performs many signs and miracles. People see the things He is doing and some even believe in His name, but then the Bible says something puzzling, "But Jesus on his part did not entrust himself to them, because he knew all people" (John 2:24). I believe this is one of the most frightening passages in all the Bible. To think there were some people whom Jesus wouldn't entrust Himself to, even though they believed in Him. What could be the issue here? Perhaps there were many, but I will offer one. These people were not ones who would chase God's glory. They were people who would use God's glory to their own end. Remember, the nature of God's glory is that it is first and foremost all about Him, not about us.

Ask yourself this question, "Do God and I have any secrets?" We don't find, in the story of Moses, his recounting of this glory moment with other people. My wife and I have an intimate relationship. We know things about each other that other people do not know and should not know—this is information just between us. These details about each other fuel a deeper intimacy in our relationship.

Then ask yourself this, "What do I want from God?" Is it something material, financial, or in some way beneficial to you, or do you simply want more of Him? The greatest reward of the Christian life is God Himself, not some other residual blessing. Jeremiah 9:24 says, "But let him who boasts boast in this, that he understands and knows me, that I am the Lord who practices steadfast love, justice, and righteousness in the earth. For in these things I delight, declares the Lord." When we settle in our minds and hearts that the great reward of faith is Him, then we can become the glory chasers He desires.

God's glory is good. God tells Moses, "I will make all my goodness pass before you and will proclaim before you my name." It's interesting that Moses asks God to show him His glory and God refers to His glory as goodness. Remember, God is working for His glory and your good, and His glory is powerful. God tells Moses, "But . . . you cannot see my face, for no one shall see me and live." God's glory causes things to happen. It changes people and places. His glory is His divine weight leveraged in the world and in our lives.

    When we see God's glorious power manifested in our midst, it changes us. One day on a mountain, Jesus manifested the glory of God that was contained in Himself to his inner circle—Peter, James, and John. Matthew 17 gives the details of the encounter:

> After six days Jesus took with him Peter, James and John the brother of James, and led them up a high mountain by themselves. There he was transfigured before them. His face shone like the sun, and his clothes became as white as the light. Just then there appeared before them Moses and Elijah, talking with Jesus.
>
> Peter said to Jesus, "Lord, it is good for us to be here. If you wish, I will put up three shelters—one for you, one for Moses and one for Elijah."
>
> While he was still speaking, a bright cloud covered them, and a voice from the cloud said, "This is my Son, whom I love; with him I am well pleased. Listen to him!"

> When the disciples heard this, they fell facedown to the ground, terrified. But Jesus came and touched them. "Get up," he said. "Don't be afraid." When they looked up, they saw no one except Jesus.
>
> As they were coming down the mountain, Jesus instructed them, "Don't tell anyone what you have seen, until the Son of Man has been raised from the dead." (Matt. 17:1–9, NIV)

Jesus pulls back his humanity and allows these men to see His divinity. He was "transfigured," meaning He was lit up with the glory of God. To add to the awesomeness, Moses and Elijah, from the Old Testament, show up on the mountaintop. I would say this was a unique day for these men—a very personal encounter. But notice it is when God Himself speaks from a cloud, these men "fell facedown to the ground, terrified." Now that is powerful. All of the other events did not lead to their face plant—God's voice did. You know why? God's glory is powerful. When God's glory has engulfed you, as it did these men, some incredible things happen because of God's glorious power. Peter even says, "Lord, it is good for us to be here." He wanted to erect some shelters so they could camp out on the mountaintop, near the glory of God. God's glory makes you long for more of it. However, God reveals His glory not so we can stay on the mountaintop but so that we can live life back down the mountain. God gave Peter, James, and a John a glimpse of His goodness, His glory, because He knew they were going to need it in the days ahead. Peter becomes the preacher of Pentecost, who leads thousands of people to faith in Christ. James becomes the first leader of the church. John will write a book in the New Testament. Ironically, each of them pays with their lives for chasing God's glory, but He is worth it.

To me one of the greatest characteristics missing in most churches is a lack of power. And I am not talking about willpower because if that was enough, most of us would be a few pounds thinner. I am talking about the power associated with His glory. First Corinthians 4:20 says, "For the kingdom of God does not consist in talk but in power." We have more programs in churches today than ever. For any problem in life, we have a program to fix it—your marriage, your money, your delinquent kids. You name it, we got it. Many people lead defeated lives, often wondering to themselves, *Is this as good as it gets?* You know why churches end up settling on programs? Because they have given up receiving His presence that gives us His power. Since God is working for His own glory, when we endeavor in the same labor, unexplainable realities ought to occur, and this is for our good. His presence would fix many of our problems if we would seek His glory.

But, better yet, God's glory is good because we are protected by it. Remember, God tells Moses, "Behold, there is a place by me where you shall stand on the rock, and while my glory passes by I will put you in a cleft of the rock, and I will cover you with my hand until I have passed by. Then I will take away my hand, and you shall see my back, but my face shall not be seen." You and I are never more secure than when we experience the powerful presence of the glory of God. When we are in His presence, we can be confident. Notice God was not going to overwhelm Moses; he was going to put Moses in the notch of a rock and then only allow Moses to see his back, or His hind parts. This is a little bit funny. God knows that His face will kill Moses, but Moses could handle the glory just associated with His hind parts.

When we experience God's glorious presence, we are protected to do whatever He might ask us to do. We have a "holy swagger" that gives us confidence for all we do—even die. What? I have always wondered how some people are able to, seemingly supernaturally, take great risks with God. Notice, I said *with* God, not *for* God; there is a big difference. I can't do anything for God. Apart from Him I can do nothing, but with Him I have limitless potential and confidence because He is always working for His own glory (John 15:5). I have the ability to deal with and endure the best and darkest of days.

Do you remember the story of Stephen, the first martyr in the book of Acts? He preaches a convicting message to the people, and they turn on him, wanting to stone him. The Bible says of Stephen, "But Stephen, full of the Holy Spirit, looked up to heaven and saw the glory of God, and Jesus standing at the right hand of God" (Acts 7:55, NIV). Stephen did not have a death wish, but He was protected, even unto death, by the glory of God.

What will the glory of God cause you to do? I can promise you this—you don't experience the glory of God and stay the same. Friend, don't settle for anything but His presence. Let your prayer be that of Moses, "Show me your glory!"

Two Warnings about Glory

You might be thinking, *I agree with what has been written, but I really don't want to do this or live this way.* Then I would simply say you are delaying the good God intends for His glory to bring to your life. He works for His glory and your good. Delaying living for God's glory only hurts you. And here is the real danger: the more success you experience in this life, the easier it is to start chasing your own glory.

Notice what happened to King Nebuchadnezzar. He began to chase his own glory. He was a great king in Babylon. He created a city of wonder that no one else had ever conceived. Who hasn't heard of the Hanging Gardens of Babylon?[2] He was a remarkable man. The problem was he started to believe that about himself. He began to chase his own glory. Nebuchadnezzar said of himself, "Is not this great Babylon, which I have built by my mighty power as a royal residence and for the glory of my majesty?" (Dan. 4:30). This was a bad idea. Chasing your own glory never works out well. Notice what happens: "While the words were still in the king's mouth, there fell a voice from heaven, 'O King Nebuchadnezzar, to you it is spoken: The kingdom has departed from you, and you shall be driven from among men, and your dwelling shall be with the beasts of the field. And you shall be made to eat grass like an ox, and seven periods of time shall pass over you, until you know that the Most High rules the kingdom of men and gives it to whom he will" (Dan. 4:31–32).

For seven years the greatest leader in the known world lived outside with the animals, eating grass and out of his mind. This sounds far-fetched, doesn't it? Not really. Feeding our own ego, living for ourselves, chasing our own glory will make us do things and end up in places we never thought possible. We live outside God's intended plan for us. Remember, God's glory is good for us. It gives us purpose, meaning, and clear direction.

Fortunately for Nebuchadnezzar things turned around. The story concludes: "At the end of the days I, Nebuchadnezzar, lifted my eyes to heaven, and my reason returned to me, and I blessed the Most High, and praised and honored him who lives forever, for his dominion is an everlasting dominion, and his kingdom endures from generation to generation; all the inhabitants of the earth are accounted as nothing, and he does according to his will among the host of heaven and among the inhabitants of the earth; and none can stay his hand or say to him, 'What have you done?'" (Dan. 4:34–35).

God was so good to Nebuchadnezzar that He let his reason return to him. As soon as the king got his mind back, he immediately began to extol the glory of God. Nebuchadnezzar figures out what all of life is about—God's glory and his good.

What about you? Have you come to your senses yet? Perhaps you have been living in a rough season, just like this ancient king. One day things seem great, and then your world comes crashing down. Whose glory have you been chasing? Perhaps today is the day of reason returning to you?

You might be asking, "What is the worst thing that could happen to me if I simply keep chasing my own glory?" Well, I can tell you this—life does not end well. The book of Acts includes a short story about a king named Herod. The people of two cities, Tyre and Sidon, depended on Herod for their food supply. They had made Herod angry, and they were worried about their security. So they asked for a meeting with him, and at the appointed meeting the people began to play to Herod's ego. They made him feel like he was ten feet tall. The Bible gives more detail: "On an appointed day Herod put on his royal robes, took his seat upon the throne, and delivered an oration to them. And the people were shouting, 'The voice of a god, and not of a man!' Immediately an angel of the Lord struck him down, *because he did not give God the glory*, and he was eaten by worms and breathed his last" (Acts 12:21–23).

Herod did not give God glory, and God destroyed him—he was eaten by worms. I don't think Hollywood could have come up with a more dramatic ending. Here is the reality—people who insist on chasing their own glory destroy themselves. This kind of glory chaser ends up in hell with all the others who throughout time have sought and fought for their own glory.

What choice do you and I really have other than to become aggressive chasers of God's glory? God is for God. God is all about His glory. The irony is, His glory is the thing we need the most. His glory brings about our greatest good. Live with a relentless pursuit of His glory!

Questions

1. How are God's glory and your good related?
2. Whose glory are you chasing?
3. How can God get glory in you today?

Chapter 4
Forsaking Glory

Why is the world so messed up? When you throw that question out to the masses, you get a lot of Monday morning quarterbacks. Some will say we need tougher laws to deal with lawbreakers, but the reality is, we have created elaborate judicial systems and prisons aimed at rehabilitating offenders, which have failed. You can't make people's hearts change. A killer, a robber, a rapist, a thief remain such unless something significant happens in the core of who they are. Some have suggested that lawmakers need to pass tougher laws to prevent crime. This seems like a good idea, but one can't legislate the behavior of men to do anything. Without something greater, people will continue to do as they always have, and even worse.

Still, some might suggest that what is needed is to change the educational paradigm. If people were just armed with more knowledge, we would see a greater enlightenment in the minds of people, and this would be the silver bullet to end all our ills. The truth is, more people attend colleges in the United States today than ever, and spring break is more carnal than ever. We have generations of really well-educated sinners who just have become more sophisticated in their indulgences.

Many look to family as the place to put Humpty Dumpty back together again. If moms would be moms and dads would be dads, everything could get fixed. The problem is, no one can now agree on what constitutes a family. Some families today have two moms and two dads. Some families don't even have a mom and dad who are married. We can't even figure out how to define a home anymore. Some say we should just be accepting of everyone. If everyone would let bygones be bygones, we could all coexist. While this utopian ideal sounds good, it has never held up during any time in the history of the world.

Could it not be the reason we find ourselves so messed up as a people is due to our rejection of God's glory? Remember, God is relentless in His own exaltation, and consequently His glory is for our greatest good. I would submit to you that the problems of our day are linked directly to the outright rejection of God's glory in our midst. We, collectively, have forsaken His glory, and now we deal with the consequences.

Moving Away

This is not a new problem. It started in the book of Genesis when Adam and Eve chose to chase their own glory instead of God's when the serpent, or the devil, convinced them they could be like God, or have their own glory be equal to God's own glory, "For God knows that when you eat of it your eyes will be opened, and you will be like God, knowing good and evil" (Gen. 3:5). Interesting, how this sin was birthed long before the devil led the couple astray. Mark Sayers says it well: "Adam is physically present during the exchange with the serpent, yet for some reason, he has internally withdrawn. Adam is created by God to be engaged in relationship, primarily with God, then with Eve, and then creation. It was Adam's passivity in these key relationships that creates the ground for withdrawal. Once one withdraws from relationship the potential for objectification arises. God's goodness can be questioned when one has withdrawn, creation can be used as a tool for personal advancement when one has begun to hold it at a distance. Adam can only let the serpent tempt and mislead his wife when he has emotionally and mentally withdrawn."[3]

Individually, each one of us will fall when we become passive and withdrawn in our relationship with God. It is essential that God's glory is propelling us forward. If we ever quit being inspired and impressed by the glory of God, we will have real problems personally and corporately.

When people have become passive toward God and withdrawn, they naturally pull away from Him. They get far from His glory. After the fall of Adam and Eve, they are forced out of the garden of Eden because the holiness of God will not tolerate the profane, the dirty, or the sinful in His midst. The permanent means to salvation, ultimately through Christ, has not yet occurred. So God forces them out. I don't know this for sure, but I imagine Adam and Eve stayed as close to the garden of Eden as possible, hoping against hope that they would once again have a relationship with God, like before.

I can relate. When I was in high school, I met the love of my life, Amy. We met when I was a junior and she was a senior in high school. We dated for a few months; then Amy started college. In my ignorance and ineptitude, I broke up with her on our one-year anniversary. I thought that perhaps there was something or someone better. Had I known I had already met the only truly fulfilling and satisfying woman I would ever need, I would have never broken up with her. But I was stupid, a mere man, a mortal, a sinner, who got passive in his all-sufficient relationship, and we broke up.

Over the next few years, I kept Amy close. On college breaks I would often call, and we would go out for dinner. Yet we did not get back together until one holiday. Planning to run my same MO, I called her to go out on a date. Her mother informed me that she was with a "friend." I had a feeling this "friend" was of the male persuasion. My hackles went up. I needed to act fast. I began to do surveillance on her house, waiting for an opportunity to pounce. Some might call this stalking, but back in that era there were no stalking laws. Sure enough this would-be "friend" was indeed a male, although his maleness was called into question due to his yellow truck. Men in Texas do not drive yellow trucks, or at least they shouldn't. As soon as the "friend" left, I immediately took the opportunity to reestablish a relationship with Amy and am happy to report we have been married for nearly twenty years. And I can only pray that somewhere out there that dude got a more masculine truck.

If you want a relationship with God, you must stay close to Him. Notice what the subsequent generations of Adam and Eve did. They built a tower at a place called Babel. The Bible says the city was east of Eden (Gen. 11:1). Eden was the last place where man and God had had a relationship. Why would man want to move farther away from God? It is simple: Satan tries to push each generation farther and farther away from God's glory. Jesus said of Satan, "The thief comes only to steal and kill and destroy; I have come that they may have life, and have it to the full" (John 10:10, NIV). He wants to move people farther away from God, just like himself. Remember, Satan was ousted from heaven because he wanted to chase his own glory. The prophet Isaiah says of Satan's fall: "How you have fallen from heaven, morning star, son of the dawn! You have been cast down to the earth, you who once laid low the nations! You said in your heart, 'I will ascend to the heavens; I will raise my throne above the stars of God; I will sit enthroned on the mount of assembly, on the utmost heights of Mount Zaphon. I will ascend above the tops of the clouds; I will make myself like the Most High.' But you are brought down to the realm of the dead, to the depths of the pit" (Isa. 14:12–15).

Satan wanted to chase his own glory. He literally sat in the presence of God, and he desired to raise his own throne above God's throne. How delusional, yet how common. Knowing His own ultimate defeat, Satan continues to push people east of Eden. Of the people of Babel, the Bible says: "And they said to one another, 'Come, let us make bricks, and burn them thoroughly.' And they had brick for stone, and bitumen for mortar. Then they said, 'Come, let us build ourselves a city and a tower with its top in the heavens, and let us make a name for ourselves, lest we be dispersed over the face of the whole earth'" (Gen. 11:3–4).

These people were going to use their own ingenuity to make a name for themselves. They were going to chase their own glory, as far away from God as possible. Interesting that they would "make bricks" instead of using the natural resources God had provided them in the rocks around them. These people did not want God's help in any way, shape, or form. This describes, in many ways, the angst people have in our time toward God. Many today not only want to move far away from God, but they don't want acknowledgment or help from any deity. They want to use their own bricks to build their own "towers," to make their own names. Rabbi Jonathan Sacks says: "The builders of Babel were in effect saying: we are going to take the place of God. We are not going to respond to His law or respect His boundaries, not going to accept His Otherness. We are going to create an environment where we rule, not Him, where the Other is replaced by Self."[4]

Eastbound and Down

So, how far east of Eden are we today? How much of the glory of God have we rejected? Once people reject God and move east of Eden, they naturally descend in their behaviors. We start heading eastbound and down. Chasing the glory of God always calls us up to a holy standard. Chasing our glory results in a downward spiral of depravity. Romans 1 gives us the clearest understanding to this eastbound and downward trend. The Bible says:

For the wrath of God is revealed from heaven against all ungodliness and unrighteousness of men, who by their unrighteousness suppress the truth. For what can be known about God is plain to them, because God has shown it to them. For his invisible attributes, namely, his eternal power and divine nature, have been clearly perceived, ever since the creation of the world, in the things that have been made. So they are without excuse. For although they knew God, they did not honor him as God or give thanks to him, but they became futile in their thinking, and their foolish hearts were darkened. Claiming to be wise, *they became fools, and exchanged the glory* of the immortal God for images resembling mortal man and birds and animals and creeping things. (Rom. 1:18–23)

Heading eastbound and down begins when God is rejected. We begin to reject His standard of truth, what He has said, through His Word, the Bible, and His Son Jesus. The text says, "The wrath of God," meaning the punishment or retribution of God is coming for people who "suppress the truth." God's wrath is not abusive; it is an expression of His love. He did not just wake up on the wrong side of the universe. If someone were trying to destroy your creation, you would bring some wrath. God's love and His wrath are like the two sides of the same coin. God's love brings about God's wrath.

The word *suppress* means "to hold down or hold under." People who reject God's truth attempt to hold under God's truth. They might attempt to hold it under by policies, procedures, even court rulings, but they can't suppress His ultimate truth. Have you ever taken a beach ball to the pool and tried to hold it under the water? It doesn't work very well, does it? You can hold it under for a while, but eventually it comes bursting through the surface, sometimes popping you in the nose upon its violent exodus. Make no mistake about it, God has clearly revealed His truth in His Word and through His Son—it will not be held back.

Rejecting God's Truth

This rejection of truth is rooted in two things. The first is "ungodliness." This means "not honoring God" or "living like there is no God." There are people who get up every day and live like there is no God. Nothing they do is informed by a God awareness—they reject His truth! They are quickly headed eastbound and down, chasing their own glory. Many times people live like there is no God because they do not want to be accountable for their actions and lifestyles. There is a real danger in this. Angelina Jolie was asked, when doing an interview for the movie *Atlas*, whether there is a god. She replied: "For the people who believe in it, I hope so. There doesn't need to be a God for me."[5] Jolie is a wonderful humanitarian and adoptive parent. It could be argued she has done more than most people of any faith system. However, you can do really good things, not believe in the true God, and still be completely self-centered, living like there is no God.

Second, this rejection of God's truth is rooted in the "unrighteousness of men," meaning "a lack of regard for people." This refers to people who have no regard for others. Not only do they deny the glory of God, but they live with no regard for others who have been made in God's image. They want no vestige of God. While this is most readily recognized in some of the world's most sinister criminals—Ted Bundy, Jeffrey Dahmer, and others—it's harder to see, yet just as common in the office cubicle or the carpool line. People who reject God's truth live with themselves at the center of their world. The world, and everyone in it, revolves around them.

And here is the rub: God is bringing wrath down on these people. It is like the old-school Western movies where the sheriff organizes a posse to round up the bad guys. Evil will have its season for a time, but then the reckoning is coming. You reach a point when you simply must do what God says to do because He is God. Life in every area must be defined by what God says and not what you say. When you lose confidence in the truth of God's Word, you head eastbound and down.

This lack of confidence in the truth of God's Word has been ever growing over a span of about the last sixty years. Max Stiles wrote that the Greatest Generation, my grandparent's generation, accepted God's truth wholeheartedly. Their generation grew up in church and Christendom, all the vestiges of the church, and both had a huge effect on the world. Some harken back to the 1950s as the golden age of the church in America. Its influence and power were second to none. Then, in my parents' generation, the baby boomers, the truth of God was assumed. Since this generation was largely churched, having been dragged to church by their parents, people assumed this generation embraced the truth of God. This was not true. The baby boomers in general chased their own glory—taking selfishness and freedom to greater extreme. My generation, the Xers, learned a confused truth about God from their parents. We learned a spirituality that had some roots in the Bible but just as many from Oprah Winfrey's latest guest. Basically most of my generation learned a truth that said, "Be good"—whatever *good* means. Now my generation has produced the millennial generation who have largely rejected God's truth.[6] Thom Rainer, president of LifeWay, says about this population of young adults, born between 1980 and 2000: only 15 percent of them believe in the truth of the gospel of Jesus Christ.[7] With each generation, culture has continued farther eastbound and down.

Rejecting God's Person

Rejecting God continues to a greater degree, not just by rejecting His truth but also rejecting His person. God is a person, not a thing, an energy, or an "it." He is a person—with personality. So He is not "the Man upstairs" or "the Big Guy" or any other impersonal idea that gets thrown out. God is a person, and He takes it personally when His glory is robbed. How many of you have ever been dumped by someone you dated? I bet you did not take that well. No one likes to be replaced.

God absolutely discloses Himself to all people through natural revelation. The text says, "For what can be known about God is plain to them. . . . For his invisible attributes, namely, His eternal power and divine nature, have clearly been perceived. . . . So they are without excuse" (Rom. 1:19–20). God is clearly seen in nature. A few years ago our faith family adopted an unreached people group in an Asian country. I had the opportunity to visit these people and heard the testimony of a young girl who was saved. She is one of the few people who are saved out of a people group of eight million people.[8] She grew up in one of the most famous mountain ranges in the world. She said as a child, before accepting the truth of God's Word, she would look at the stars at night and the mountains in the daytime, and she knew that someone had made them both. She would plead, in her prayer, that whoever was behind this awesome creation would reveal Himself to her. Years later, and through persistent prayer, God showed His glory and revealed His truth to her through some missionaries. God is clearly seen in nature so that man is without excuse. The trouble is man chases his own glory with such vigor, he rarely notices the majesty of God in nature.

And once people reject God's truth and His person, they simply replace Him. People naturally chase after something or someone. Don't believe me? Ask them. Everyone has a reason they get up in the morning and do something. Where people put their greatest time, energy, and affection reveals who or what they are chasing. Romans 1 makes abundantly clear that people heading eastbound and down trade the glory of the Creator to chase the glory of the created. Psalm 115:8 says, "Those who make them become like them; so do all who trust in them." People will become what they bow down to, and everyone bows down to something or someone. We are wired to worship. It comes naturally for all people. Some may not think of themselves as a worshipper, but you will chase the glory of the person or thing you value most. It could be a job, a person, a lifestyle, a status, achievement, money; you become what you chase.

Redefining Morality

When God is rejected, morality gets redefined. If people don't get the God part right, they will not get anything else right. They will chase the wrong thing with the wrong standard. Everyone has a standard for right and wrong—it does not matter who you are or where you are from. When there is not a clear standard for everyone, like God's truth the Bible, people have to develop their own standard. This begins by corrupt thinking. Remember, if you are not chasing the glory of God, you are chasing your own glory, and you are now the object of your narcissism. So morality begins to get redefined by "corrupt thinking." The text says, "Claiming to be wise, they became fools" (Rom. 1:22). When we reject God and redefine morality, we will always be weak thinkers because we cannot outthink God. First Corinthians 1:25 says, "For the foolishness of God is wiser than men, and the weakness of God is stronger than men." When we chase our own glory, we will justify things we want to justify because we are satisfying our own narcissism.

But it gets worse: corrupt thinking leads to corrupt actions. Romans 1:24–27 says: "Therefore God gave them up in the lusts of their hearts to impurity, to the dishonoring of their bodies among themselves, because they exchanged the truth about God for a lie and worshiped and served the creature rather than the Creator, who is blessed forever! Amen. For this reason God gave them up to dishonorable passions. For their women exchanged natural relations for those that are contrary to nature; and the men likewise gave up natural relations with women and were consumed with passion for one another, men committing shameless acts with men and receiving in themselves the due penalty for their error."

We first think things and then do things. When you see the word *therefore* in the Bible, you must always ask, "What is it there for?" A *therefore* in the Bible means everything that is about to be said is based on everything that has already been said. So, based on man's rejection of God and the redefining of truth, God gave them up—let them have their own way. It is as if God finally says, "If you want to chase your own glory, you can." The phrase "gave them up" gives the image of a stream and a canoe. God takes the canoe and lets it go downstream without any direction. Some people fear God's intervening in their lives, making them do things they don't want to do. The worst thing imaginable is what is pictured here—God takes His hand off of you, and He lets you do what you want to do. Now that is scary!

Homosexuality is used throughout this text as a clear illustration of this moving eastbound and down. I want to be careful here. It is easy for evangelical Christians to condemn homosexuals and fail to notice the much larger list of sins found later in this text. I believe homosexuality is used because it clearly presents this downward trajectory the most demonstratively. When people throw out God's standard, His Word, as the lens through which they interpret experience, they will use their experience as the lens to which they interpret truth. The latter makes me the authority. My decision making will not be based on God's glory but on pragmatism. Does this work? So, when God calls for marriage to be between a man and a woman, and if someone does not like that definition, they can simply redefine marriage in their own terms, and now the descent begins in our thinking. Essentially, if it is working, it must be true, regardless of what God says in the matter.

Actions

Quickly our actions follow our thoughts: "God gave them up in lusts of their heart to impurity, to the dishonoring of their bodies among themselves, because they exchanged the truth about God for a lie, and worshiped and served the creature rather than the Creator" (Rom. 1:24–25). Wow! See this progression? These people started doing what feels good and feels right, not what was good or right according to God's standard. I heard a comedian once tell the story of being at a traffic intersection, with a car in front of him with a sticker that says, "If it feels good, do it." So the comedian bumped the car in front of him with his car. The kid driving the car with the sticker got out and asked the comedian what he was doing. To which the comedian responded, "Just following the advice of your bumper sticker!" Obviously our feelings, to be valid, must be informed by some standard of truth. My feelings might simply be wrong. I can't act on every impulse or desire I have.

Lifestyles

Corrupt thinking and corrupt actions can only lead to one thing—corrupt lifestyles, "For this reason God gave them up to dishonorable passions. For their women exchanged natural relations for those that are contrary to nature; and the men likewise gave up natural relations with women and were consumed with passion for one another, men committing shameless acts with men and receiving in themselves the due penalty for their error" (Rom. 1:26–27). See the progression—corrupt thinking, actions, and then lifestyle. Women and men begin to do what is unnatural. Now this is unpopular today, and many, even some reading this, will simply believe I am just an uninformed simpleton. That may be, but we have reached a point where what God can't tolerate, we will, and who God gives mercy to, we won't.

I have heard many in the homosexual community argue that they were "born this way." To which I would agree—they were born that way. We were all born into sin. My family has a history of addiction and immorality. I have no doubt, apart from the work of God in my life, I would have struggled with both of these sins. When God did His saving work in me, He changed me (2 Cor. 5:17). Further, what about families where the family sin is murder or robbery. Is it OK to be a murderer or a robber? I mean if I was born this way—I can't help it, right?

Current State

Here is a nutshell of culture's current state. When you have corrupt thinking and lose truth, you get relativism. Relativism allows people to start basing truth on popular opinion or consensus building. So, if the masses deem it right, it is right. If the masses deem it wrong, it is wrong. So by today's logic two men or two women can have the same rights as traditional marriage partners because who are you to judge my version of the truth; and culture says this behavior is valid.

Then, once the standard for truth has been changed, you get corrupt actions. Corrupt actions bring tolerance. At this point in the downward trajectory, anything goes. If my corrupt actions work for me, it is none of your business. Life works on pragmatism. If it works, then it must be right. The only thing a tolerant culture cannot tolerate is intolerant people. This is why so many evangelical Christians are readily attacked for having a biblical worldview. The Bible is intolerant because God doesn't change His standard with the times.

When culture accepts corrupt lifestyles through laws and deviant behavior is openly celebrated in the streets, that culture has reached political correctness. Political correctness censors an honest conversation. Anyone who opposes the views of the tolerant will be attacked, labeled, and blackballed from the mainstream.

Refusing Repentance

Finally, cultures and people continue eastbound and down when, after rejecting God and redefining morality, they refuse repentance. Romans 1 continues: "And since they did not see fit to acknowledge God, God gave them up to a debased mind to do what ought not to be done. They were filled with all manner of unrighteousness, evil, covetousness, malice. They are full of envy, murder, strife, deceit, maliciousness. They are gossips, slanderers, haters of God, insolent, haughty, boastful, inventors of evil, disobedient to parents, foolish, faithless, heartless, ruthless. Though they know God's righteous decree that those who practice such things deserve to die, they not only do them but give approval to those who practice them" (Rom. 1:28–32).

You will notice the phrase "God gave them up to a debased mind." *Debased* is a powerful word meaning "unable to judge rightly" or "the inability to think correctly." The problem with a sin like any of these listed is that, if you refuse to repent, you lack the ability to think rightly over time. You become debased. With all of these lifestyles one runs the risk of becoming damned. You can be debased because you are disobedient to parents or faithless or haughty or a murderer.

So each of these is horrible. But the sin of homosexuality, which has spanned this text, might be the most recognizable. I have never seen a group of murderers dressed up in costumes demanding their rights, have you? I have never seen a group of gossips lobbying lawmakers for equal protection under the law, have you? I have never seen a group of pimple-faced, pubescent kids marching in the streets asking for the overthrow of their parents. But I have seen homosexuals parade, lobby, and demand their rights. Why? It might be because God has handed them over to a debased mind. Maybe we can no longer have informed conversations with people in these lifestyles because they no longer have the ability to think rightly. An unpopular opinion, I know, but could it be?

The text goes on to say that debased people "give approval to those who practice them." I do not doubt the sincerity of many in a homosexual lifestyle. I imagine they sincerely love their partners, but it is possible for a person to be sincere and sincerely be wrong.

What is gripping in this text is found in the phrase, "They . . . deserve to die." By the way, the text means all the people in this list. One sin is not greater than another, but lifestyles condemn. First Corinthians 6:9–10 (NIV) says, "Or do you not know that wrongdoers will not inherit the kingdom of God? Do not be deceived: Neither the sexually immoral nor idolaters nor adulterers nor men who have sex with men nor thieves nor the greedy nor drunkards nor slanderers nor swindlers will inherit the kingdom of God."

Down but Not Out

So, will sexually immoral people of all kinds of perversity make it to heaven? Or will people who have ever robbed someone make the cut? Or what about substance abusers, can they get into heaven? The answer is yes. But here is the condition: these people don't make these practiced lifestyles. These people don't reject God; they believe in His person. They don't redefine morality; they believe the Bible is God's holy standard and His Son is Jesus. They don't refuse to repent; rather, they fall upon the mercy of a God who, "as far as the east is from the west, so far does he remove our transgressions from us" (Ps. 103:12). Don't you see it is through the salvation that only He can bring that He stops our eastbound and downward descent and saves us for His glory so He will get the credit of our lives, and in His glory we will find our greatest good. He gives us what we need the most—Himself. We need to quit running east of Eden and back to Him.

Questions

1. How have things changed in your lifetime?

2. What is the right response for Christians toward those who practice and promote what the Bible calls sin?

3. What is your role in transforming culture?

Chapter 5
Faith Ratchets Up

Have you ever felt you were not making any progress? Maybe it has been in your job. You continue to be overlooked for upward advancement. Maybe it's your personal life. You can't find Mr. or Mrs. Right; for that matter you can't even find Mr. or Mrs. Right Now. Perhaps your family life seems to be stale with your kids or with your spouse. You might even find that you wonder if the Christian life is really the best life. You look at the pages of the Bible, and you have a difficult time seeing how it all applies to you. You might have even thought you were the only one struggling in these areas. I don't think you are alone at all. For that matter I think many people simply go through the spiritual motions and suffer, silently wondering, *Is this it?*

I'm not going to pretend for a moment that I have everything figured out. However, I can tell you, based on what the Bible says and based on my own experience, that the Christian life is never boring. If you or I get bored, it is simply due to our inability to think and act on a higher level. Do you know what I mean by that: "to think and act on a higher level"? I am not a crazy "name it and claim it" Christ follower. I am not really a very emotional person. Now I'm not a closed-off, emotional midget, friendless American male, which is pretty typical these days. As believers, we should live in a balanced state of spirit and truth. Both are essential in our relationship with Christ. I am a fairly levelheaded guy.

In my years of following Jesus, I have experienced times of trial as well as moments of turmoil and tragedy. I've had moments where I wondered how things would work out because nothing made sense to me. I've had times when I thought I might be a little crazy because what God seemed to be asking me to do made no logical sense. And in these moments I've been reminded of one thing, one characteristic of my relationship with Christ that is vastly different with Him than with any other person in my life. My relationship with Christ is based solely on faith. Solely on faith.

You may say, "Well, your other relationships depend on faith." You would be right to some degree. I have a relationship with my wife based on faithfulness. We pledged our faithfulness to each other. I have a faith relationship to my children. My kids have faith that I will take care of their needs and, to be honest, a good many of their wants. My friends have faith in me that I will be loyal to them and keep confidences when needed. However, in every one of these relationships, we can see one another in the flesh.

Calling of Faith

With Jesus everything hinges on faith. In every case faith comes as a result of the calling of Christ. "So faith comes from hearing, and hearing through the word of Christ" (Rom. 10:17). Think about it? I don't know where or how you came to know Christ, but here is what I do know: you came when Christ called. You might have heard Christ call through the sermon of some preacher. You might have had a friend or family member share Christ with you, and you heard His call. You might have been reading the Bible on your own and you heard His call. Whatever the method, Christ called you to Himself. At that moment a faith relationship began by grace through faith (Eph. 2:8).

Jesus calls each person to Himself like a shepherd does his sheep. Jesus said about Himself, "And I have other sheep that are not of this fold. I must bring them also, and they will listen to my voice. So there will be one flock, one shepherd" (John 10:16). Some voices are distinctive to our ears. I was always amazed at how my kids, as babies, would react to their mother's voice. Sometimes when we would pick our kids up from the nursery at church, my wife, Amy, could hear them crying from down the hall. Her pace would pick up to hasten her arrival to their classroom. As soon as she was in earshot, she would simply call out to our son or daughter, and immediately they would grow silent. While unable to understand much of anything, they were able to distinguish the sound of their mother's voice from all of the competing noises around them, mainly the screams of other kids. In the same way Christ calls us, and we, if we are His, hear His voice. In this way Christ must reveal Himself to us in faith.

Conferring Faith

The Bible says, "Now faith is the assurance of things hoped for, the conviction of things not seen" (Heb. 11:1). When Christ called me to faith, He also conferred faith to me. *Confer* means "to give or to bestow or to honor." So on no level did I really do anything. Faith itself is and was a gift from the beginning to the end. "For in it the righteousness of God is revealed from faith for faith, as it is written, 'The righteous shall live by faith'" (Rom. 1:17). The more I grow in my own faith, at times I am really impatient with people who do not get it. I see seemingly elementary problems that people are dealing with, and I am like, "Dude, really, move on!" The truth is, I have been given something that all Christ followers have and those who are not Christ followers do not have—faith.

This is important to remember: faith is a gift conferred on you. As I deal with people who are not Christ followers and attempt to share Christ with them, many times my words do not penetrate their understanding. In fact, on more than one occasion—and this is continuing to grow in frequency—I have people who say to me, "You really believe all of that?" Think about it: God creates the world. People sin. Sin separates people from God. God comes up with a plan. He then sends a Baby, who is His Son, into the world, through a virgin teenage girl. His Son grows up and lives a perfect life, does nothing wrong. This son, Jesus, is killed on the cross for the sins of the world. He then resurrects from the dead proving He is God. He appears to more than five hundred people, then jets back to heaven, leaving the Holy Spirit to fill people called Christians, who make up the church, to go give out the good news about this God. You have to admit, it sounds far-fetched unless God reveals this to you. The Bible says, "The natural person does not accept the things of the Spirit of God, for they are folly to him, and he is not able to understand them because they are spiritually discerned" (1 Cor. 2:14).

Conditions for Faith

So the fact that Christ has called us to faith and conferred faith upon us is nothing less than miraculous. But, if I have just stepped into this eternal relationship with Jesus, why do I not seem to be living differently? Why do I continue to struggle with the monotony of life? Why do I get overwhelmed about things that really don't even matter in light of eternity? Now here is the rub. Christ's calling us to faith and conferring faith upon us creates the conditions for us to live a life of faith. The reason many feel spiritually lethargic is due to their disconnecting of faith with obedience. This is a question of obedience. Dietrich Bonhoeffer, a

German theologian and pastor during World War II, had this to offer in answering these questions: "Obedience remains separated from faith. From the point of view of justification it is necessary thus to separate them, but we must never lose sight of their essential unity. For faith is only real where there is obedience, never without it, and only becomes faith in the act of obedience."[9]

Faith and obedience are connected like the two sides of the same coin. There is really only faith when these two dynamics are at work within you at the same time. So faith is not simply believing in the unseen or the optimistic hope of an old Billy Joel or George Michael song; it is action of belief. Hebrews 11:6 says, "And without faith it is impossible to please him, for whoever would draw near to God must believe that he exists and that he rewards those who seek him." So without belief and obedience regularly operating with one another, we can't please God.

While our faith is a gift from God to us, our works, according to the New Testament writer James, demonstrates that we have what we profess (James 2:17). This is why it seems illogical to me for people to say they have trusted Christ as Savior and Lord in the past and then lived estranged from Jesus for decades. While they may have possessed some understanding of what faith could be, they most likely didn't experience true faith because faith isn't just belief; it is proven in obedience.

Therefore, knowing that Christ has called you to faith and conferred faith upon you, the conditions for your faith to be exercised are ready, but are you willing to be obedient? If you seem stagnant in your Christian life, the question is simple, Are you obedient to everything God has called you to do? Think about it. If not, why should God reveal one more thing to you about Himself, if you are not willing to do what He has already clearly commanded? Remember, without faith it is impossible to please God. Not hard, difficult, or extremely perilous—it is impossible. It can't be done.

If you know you are disobedient in some area of your life, become obedient and prove your faith so you can please God. You will continue to sit in your stagnant, bored, tired, and pitiful state until you start "faithing." *Faith* is a verb; it is action. You will be surprised how fast things start happening when you starting faithing.

One day Peter, the fisherman and soon to be disciple of Jesus, was fishing. In fact, he fished all night with his brother and associates and caught nothing. Then Jesus stepped into his boat. Jesus could have stepped into someone else's boat, but He stepped into Peter's boat, like Jesus has discriminately stepped into your life. After He used Peter's boat for a PA system to speak to the large crowd that had come out to hear Him speak, Jesus told Peter to "put out into the deep and let down your nets for a catch" (Luke 5:4). This request defied all logic. Peter was the fisherman. What did this carpenter know about fishing? But the conditions for faithing were set, and now Peter had to make a choice, just like you. When Jesus steps into our lives, the conditions for faith are set. What will we do? Peter obeyed. See, faith not only believes; it obeys.

So, why are you not *faithing* in the areas where God has clearly revealed Himself to you? You might think to yourself, *I know I need to do this or that, but I will eventually do it.* Can I simply remind you that delayed obedience is not obedience. It is simply a passive-aggressive form of disobedience. Get to it!

In Peter's case his faith was rewarded. Remember, He (God) rewards those who seek Him (Heb. 11:1). After the nets were lowered, what came up was miraculous. Peter caught more fish than he ever had before. The conditions were right for *faithing*, and Peter responded well. His risk of faith was rewarded. We, as people, like to be rewarded. And when we think about the rewards, many things might come to your mind. Some might naturally think about physical or material things. In some cases that might be true. For others it might be some other tangible reward like position or power. Maybe it could be relational blessings. However, Scripture clearly tells us the greatest reward we receive: "The kingdom of heaven is like treasure hidden in a field, which a man found and covered up. Then in his joy he goes and sells all that he has and buys that field" (Matt. 13:44). The great prize of faith is that we get Jesus. Better still, He gets more of us. If Christ is not enough for you, then you will be sadly disappointed by the Christian life. Faith, through belief and obedience, gives us greater opportunity to see God do greater still.

Changes in Faith

Understanding that Christ calls us to faith, confers faith upon us, and allows the conditions for faith, we must also realize that faith changes—it ratchets up. What was faith for you last year or last week might not be faith for you today. Sometimes our faith stagnates because our faith is not ratcheting up. Faith grows when we use it. God is constant in His character and nature, but He reserves the right to change His methods to advance our faith.

Let's be candid—we are creatures of habit. Our default switch will always be that which is comfortable, easy, and familiar. Even the wildest risk taker will eventually choose safety. We do not like change. A man once told me, "All change is bad, even if it's good." How true. We hate change. However, for God to change our character, you will find that He often uses change itself. In fact, rarely, if ever, does God allow things in our lives to remain static. This is best demonstrated in the faith journey of the nation of Israel. There are two significant water crossings in Israel's history, and they are altogether different.

The first water crossing involved the Red Sea. Exodus 14:21–29 says:

> Then Moses stretched out his hand over the sea, and the Lord drove the sea back by a strong east wind all night and made the sea dry land, and the waters were divided. And the people of Israel went into the midst of the sea on dry ground, the waters being a wall to them on their right hand and on their left. The Egyptians pursued and went in after them into the midst of the sea, all Pharaoh's horses, his chariots, and his horsemen. And in the morning watch the Lord in the pillar of fire and of cloud looked down on the Egyptian forces and threw the Egyptian forces into a panic, clogging their chariot wheels so that they drove heavily. And the Egyptians said, "Let us flee from before Israel, for the Lord fights for them against the Egyptians."

> Then the Lord said to Moses, "Stretch out your hand over the sea, that the water may come back upon the Egyptians, upon their chariots, and upon their horsemen." So Moses stretched out his hand over the sea, and the sea returned to its normal course when the morning appeared. And as the Egyptians fled into it, the Lord threw the Egyptians into the midst of the sea. The waters returned and covered the chariots and the horsemen; of all the host of Pharaoh that had followed them into the sea, not one of them remained. But the people of Israel walked on dry ground through the sea, the waters being a wall to them on their right hand and on their left.

Several components are essential for our understanding this first *faithing* event. First, the people had a slave mentality. The Israelites had been in captivity in Egypt for over four hundred years. They had been abused mercilessly by their Egyptian masters. Moses, God's agent of freedom, shows up to lead the people out of slavery. Moses represents what Christ has ultimately done for us in freeing us from our sin and bondage. These Israelites had no idea who God was and what He could do. They were utterly dependent on God to rescue them from their bondage. They had an infantile understanding about God and were characterized by great fear.

Children are afraid. I remember, as a kid, I slept with an army of stuffed animals. I had a stack of stuffed animals on one side of me and another stack of stuffed animals on the other side of me. I was scared of every little bump I heard in the night. My parents were constantly attempting to reassure me that everything was all right, but I did not believe them. It took time and, on their part, great patience. And so it was with God in His patience in dealing with Israel and with us.

Then, notice, God does it all. Moses stretches out his arm and "the Lord drove the sea back by a strong east wind and made the sea dry land." This miracle did not depend in any way, shape, or form on the Israelites. They were not required to do anything to make the waters part. In fact, they were powerless to do it. They stood back and watched as God did what only God can do. They simply had to step onto the dry ground, which God created out of the sea floor, and walk across to the other side.

I have experienced this firsthand. I have prayed with people who were told by doctors that their illness was terminal. And, in fact, based on the scans and tests, in every one of these cases, the doctors were correct—the patient should die. Then, through what can only be described as the supernatural hand of God, the patient lived. The scans and tests changed. Only God could have done this. God still does miracles in this supernatural way.

Later in Israel's history there is another water crossing, a second *faithing* event. Just as dramatic but altogether different. Notice the details in Joshua 3:14–17:

> So when the people set out from their tents to pass over the Jordan with the priests bearing the ark of the covenant before the people, and as soon as those bearing the ark had come as far as the Jordan, and the feet of the priests bearing the ark were dipped in the brink of the water (now the Jordan overflows all its banks throughout the time of harvest), the waters coming down from above stood and rose up in a heap very far away, at Adam, the city that is beside Zarethan, and those flowing down toward the Sea of the Arabah, the Salt Sea, were completely cut off. And the people passed over opposite Jericho. Now the priests bearing the ark of the covenant of the Lord stood firmly on dry ground in the midst of the Jordan, and all Israel was passing over on dry ground until all the nation finished passing over the Jordan.

Much has occurred since the first water crossing for the people of Israel. First, they are not the same people at all. In fact, the earlier generation, who was in bondage in Egypt, had died off. Now we find a people who have walked with God in the desert for four decades. They have the words of God through the Ten Commandments. They have seen God meet their physical needs through manna, quail, and water. They have seen His pillars of fire and cloud, assuring them of His presence. They have moved from people with a slave mentality based in fear to a people who truly belong to God.

Surely the same can be said for many of you reading this. If you are new to faith, you might be more like the Israelites mentioned earlier. Nothing wrong with that—just keep moving forward in your faith. But I suspect many reading this have walked with God for a number of years. Like these Israelites you know God better today than ever.

Then notice how this miracle gets accomplished. The first time God did all the work. This time He requires the priests, carrying the ark, to dip their feet into the water. Don't miss that detail. Nothing happened until the priests exercised enough faith to step into the water. Belief brings about obedience, which is faith. God was not going to do this for them again. They had to get out in the water before He acted.

Takeaway

The reason many of our lives, and especially churches, never see God do any more than He has done is due to our faith not ratcheting up. I am blessed to serve a church where faith has ratcheted up over the last decade. There are numerous stories of how we have had to get into the water before God moved. Let me indulge in one story.

All churches need money to operate. I don't know why people get funny when you talk about money in the church, but they do. No one gets offended about money when they come with the check at the end of your meal when you dine out. No one gets offended about money when they pay their mortgage, and no one seems to get too bent out of shape when they pay for their children's excessive extracurricular activities. Sometimes in churches, like in homes, we think our security is found in money.

In the past I have seen God do some incredible things in the area of His churches' finances. Unfortunately it didn't seem like He really knew what He was doing in this particular season.

Then, oddly enough, out of nowhere the Holy Spirit began to convict me about this reality, and it just so happened we, as a church, were chasing a budget. Like many churches in that season, the economy was rough and so were our offerings. But Easter was approaching and with it the hope of large crowds, many decisions for Christ, and a significant offering. Then, out of the blue, the Holy Spirit simply said to me, "Give away the Easter offering to other agencies that share the gospel. Don't keep a dime of the Easter offering in the church." Immediately I began to think, *Now was that really the Holy Spirit saying that, or was that indigestion?* I mean, it did not make sense. However, I was continually nagged by this undeniable compulsion to take this step of faith. So I shared this idea with our staff team. They seemed in agreement with the move. I kept hoping one of them would have a red flag, but nope. So we took the idea to our finance and personnel teams. I figured if anyone would stop it, it would be those teams. I mean, church people love security. But everyone was in agreement that we should do this. Then our deacon body was introduced to the idea. I figured out of a group of deacons, one old, gnarled, bitter soul would raise his head, but nothing except excitement filled the room. What was wrong with all of these people?

So that Easter weekend, we had the Big Give, as we called it. Wouldn't you know it? We had the largest single offering in the history of the church. Had we kept the money, we would have not only wiped out the budget deficit; we would have pulled ahead in our giving. I must admit, while I knew that faith required my belief and my obedience, I was not really that thrilled. But week after week following Easter, we continued to give money away to various organizations. And week after week, our finances got tighter and tighter.

At this point I was scheduled to go on vacation with my family. As a rule, we staff members try not to bother one another on vacation. I was sitting on the beach and, I must admit, thinking about the financial situation back home. Then my phone rang. It was our executive pastor. Being the great man of faith that I am, I thought to myself, *Great, what has gone wrong?* When I answered, he said, "I don't want to bother you." To which I am thinking, *Then why did you?* He continued, "But I want you know about something that has just happened. We have been contacted about an estate that is being settled. An elderly man, the husband of a couple who were in the church before you arrived, has just passed away. The church is going to receive an estimated $250,000." I sat in silence. He said, "Are you there?" Faith always ratchets up. God did it again in a way only He could do it. In the end it really had nothing to do with money and everything to do with seeing God come through again.

I don't know what faith ratcheting up will look like in the future, but I know that it will. For those of us whom Christ has called to faith, and conferred faith upon, know that the conditions for faith are set, and faith will change for you in the future. God desires that our faith be constantly in Him. And why should it be any other way, for He is our great reward. The funny thing is, it doesn't even require that much faith to see great things happen. Remember what Jesus said, "And the Lord said, 'If you had faith like a grain of mustard seed, you could say to this mulberry tree, "Be uprooted and planted in the sea," and it would obey you'" (Luke 17:6). Ratchet up your faith and watch Him change the world. Get to *faithing*!

Questions

1. When were you called into faith?
2. What conditions are right in your life, or the life of your church, for God to do what only God can do?
3. How has faith ratcheted up for you or your church?

Chapter 6
There Is No Glory in the Expected

Back in the day, around junior high and high school, I had the privilege of knowing the most unusual man. In this era everyone wanted to be well rounded. So, an overachiever, I played sports, was a member of several clubs, and was a member of my school choir. The man's name was Duane D. Golhke; he was my choir teacher. Golhke was about six feet three inches, always had an Abraham Lincoln type beard of fiery red hair. Golhke didn't put up with a lot of stuff from much of anyone, especially his students. Yet his toughness gave way to moments of tenderness with his students. He had high expectations for his students. He demanded their best. Choir was not simply a place to get a fine art credit to graduate; it was his life. I always marveled at the fact he never took a lunch break. He intentionally organized his classes to work through lunch. He didn't have time to catch up on the gossip of the teachers' lounge; he was all business with his students.

One year our choir was to perform in a spring choir competition in a city about sixty miles away. Golhke was not going to be riding on the death trap known as the school bus because he was already at the competition with other choirs. Other than a bus driver, we were going to be riding the bus unchaperoned. He figured, as juniors and seniors in high school, we could handle it; this was his expectation. The day before we left, he vehemently told our class that there would absolutely be no talking of any kind on the bus because we needed to save our voices for the competition. For whatever reason I took it upon myself to be the unofficial policeman of the trip. Before everyone entered the bus, I reminded them to "shut up" for the duration of our ride. I have a feeling people would have done this without my chiding, but I had taken it upon myself to ride roughshod over this herd of bozos.

We were off. I popped my head above the rather large high-backed, uncomfortable, pleather seats, looking for would-be rule breakers. Any time someone attempted to lower a window, I quickly ran to raise it—Golhke said "to keep the windows up because the wind could dry out our voices." Not only did I raise windows, but I attempted to shoot my classmates looks of utter disappointment in order to shame them into repentance.

When all was said and done, we arrived at our competition without a hitch. To be honest, as I came off the bus last, making sure everyone was quiet to the bitter end, I felt that whatever score we received that day would in some way be due to my self-appointed sheriffing of these simpletons I called classmates. As I stepped off the bus, Golhke's rather regal Abe Lincoln-like self was there, all six feet three inches of him. Without any solicitation, I proudly said, "Mr. Golhke, we made it from home, no one talked, and the windows remained up the entire time." Now I was looking for some grand comment of affirmation. I figured he would extol my greatness. I mean, surely, he of all people must understand how hard it is to corral a group of hormonal teenagers—artists on top of that. We all know they are a little more kooky than the average person.

But, much to my chagrin, Golhke looked at me and said some words that have stayed with me for a lifetime. He said, "Kris, there is no glory in the expected." *What!* I thought to myself, *There is no glory in the expected—what did that mean?* Had he just run a Jedi mind trick on me? It was like a magician who pulled the rabbit out of his hat and I never saw it coming or being the punch line of a joke I didn't understand. No glory in the expected?

Gohlke was striking at the heart of my entitlement—the belief that I deserved something because I did what I should do. In one statement he completely deconstructed my belief system. We live in an entitled world. People believe they deserve things they have never worked for or earned. We live in an overly incentivized world where kids get trophies for just showing up and people get free cell phones for doing nothing. I've heard of a high school this past year that had more than twenty valedictorians.

No one will want to admit this, but many times, if not most of the time, many people believe God must give us something because we display some form of nominal obedience. Many people live under the false belief that attending a church about 50 percent of the time, giving a little money—not a tithe but a tip—and doing some nominal volunteer work will be enough to keep this completely narcissistic, self-obsessed, glory-seeking God of the Bible happy enough with our conduct that He will be forced to bless us and keep us disease free. We desire to put God in our debt. This is a bad plan. It never works. You can never, in a thousand lifetimes, come close to doing something big enough that God would owe you something. The fact that He works in us is a credit to Him, not us. He gets glory from you by working through you. If there is any good in you, it is because He put it there. To this understanding I would say, like my old teacher, "There is no glory in the expected!" God expects our lives to be 100 percent to His glory.

Cheap and Costly Grace

Dietrich Bonhoeffer, the German preacher and theologian, said this, "When Christ calls a man, he bids him come and die."[10] Christ gave His whole life for the Father's glory and your good. Now the expectation is that you give your whole life for Father's glory, knowing that it works for your good. Following Christ and giving God glory in all things will cost you everything. A false version of Christianity is being passed off as authentic in many quasi-faith circles. Bonhoeffer called this "cheap grace." Grace, biblical grace, is God's unmerited favor toward Christ followers. Christ followers do not receive what they deserve, which is death and hell because of their sins—that would be justice. Christ followers do not just receive the acquittal of punishment for what they have done—that would be mercy. No, Christians are lavished with the unmerited, unearned grace of God.

Cheap grace, as Bonhoeffer taught it, means we understand grace as a doctrine, principle, or system. Cheap grace teaches a concept about God but never treats God as a person with personality. This perverse grace justifies sin without justifying the sinner. We give ourselves this form of grace. This is why many people can listen to sermon after sermon, year after year, and never be affected. Cheap grace is the plight of the Western church. Any grace that does not change the way you live is no grace at all. Cheap grace is grace without the cross, without discipleship, without Jesus Christ, who is alive.

Bonhoeffer goes on to explain that costly grace is what is needed. It is costly because there is a price to pay if we are really going to follow Christ and, thus, give God the glory He demands. It is costly because it costs you your entire life. It will cost you everything. God does not operate on a time-share plan; He demands every part of you. He is not content to be a Sunday friend or a fallback lover. He demands complete, undivided priority. Yet it is grace, Bonhoeffer explains, because it gives a man what can only be called true life.[11] His grace gives the true Christ follower the ability to embrace the best and worst of moments in life to the glory of God.

Bonhoeffer, early in his writings and ministry, had no idea how he would die. It would be at the orders of the madman Adolf Hitler. Bonhoeffer was a part of a coupe to overthrow the Nazi dictator for his extermination of the Jewish people through the Holocaust. Interesting that a preacher would become an assassin. However, Bonhoeffer's belief in the equality of all men, in this case the Jews, formed by his understanding of creation, led him to this conclusion. He believed the Jews were not inferior but rather were created in the image of God. The plot to kill Hitler was unsuccessful, and in time Bonhoeffer and his coconspirators were discovered and imprisoned. For nearly eighteen months he was detained in a military prison, later to be moved to a concentration camp at the order of Hitler himself. Just hours before his death, he led his final church service for the others prisoners.[12] On April 9, 1945, at the age of thirty-nine, he was executed at Flossenburg Concentration Camp. One of his former students, Eberhard Bethge, described Bonhoeffer's final moments: "I saw Pastor Bonhoeffer . . . kneeling on the floor praying fervently to God. I was most deeply moved by the way this lovable man prayed, so devout and so certain that God heard his prayer. At the place of execution, he again said a short prayer and then climbed the few steps to the gallows, brave and composed. His death ensued after a few seconds. In the almost fifty years that I worked as a doctor, I have hardly ever seen a man die so entirely submissive to the will of God."[13]

Where has this type of uncompromised, wholehearted discipleship gone? My concern for many contemporary Christians is that we have gotten Jesus just the way we like Him—efficient, manageable, and on demand. We have failed to understand the incredible magnitude of the demands of discipleship—and this is not optional—where some people will do this and others will not. This demand has not changed. The danger of the church in the West is like Christians in Nazi Germany, who had a rich religious history. After all Germany gave the world Martin Luther and the Reformation. They had a form of religion, but they did not really know Jesus. The problem with a country that has a rich religious history is that faith becomes cultural and even at times sentimental. This is why Christmas and Easter still draw big crowds in the United States, but faith ceases to be consequential.

Some might look at a man like Bonhoeffer and think his version of Christianity seems a bit extreme. Really? Have you looked in the pages of Scripture lately? Do you see any well-adjusted people in the Bible? People who were real suburban? I read the stories of people who fought giants, defied kings, risked their lives to preach the gospel, went face-to-face with evil. What I do not see are any well-adjusted people. I see no people who were well received and conventional. Could it be that what we possess today and call "Christianity" would look really abnormal to those whom the stories of the Bible are written about? Could it be that the words of men and women of the Bible, and people like Bonhoeffer, would look at our contemporized version of "churchianity" and say, "There is no glory in the expected"?

Deny, Take, and Follow

Jesus made a declaration to His would-be followers, "If anyone would come after me, let him deny himself and take up his cross daily and follow me" (Luke 9:23). This has always been the litmus test for glory chasers. In the days leading up to the epic battle of the Alamo, Commander William Barrett Travis informed the courageous fighters of the mission that the army of Santa Anna was increasing in number and no help was going to come for the battle. With dramatic flair he drew his sword, drew a line in the sand, and asked his men to make a decision. If you want to stay and fight, step across the line. If you want to leave, stay where you are. Many now immortalized men like James Bowie and Davy Crockett stepped across that line, knowing they had just surrendered their lives. In the same way Jesus expects true disciples to step across the proverbial line. For some reason many well-intentioned Christians do not realize this today. Again, there is no glory in the expected.

Jesus said we are to deny ourselves. The word *deny* means "to forsake self for the benefit of another." Most specifically, we deny ourselves for the sake of God's glory. Self-denial is so difficult in our on-demand, your-way-right-away kind of world. Frankly we deny ourselves little. Hudson Taylor said, "The real secret of an unsatisfied life lies too often in an unsurrendered will."[14] Many Christians do not fully experience all the benefits of this temporary life or eternal life that is already activated in them because they are not fully surrendered to either world. For one to experience the full benefit of this world, one must throw off every encumbrance that hinders optimum fulfillment—eat, drink, and be merry, for tomorrow you might die. Many believers know enough about discipleship that they will not give into every carnal desire they might possess. Yet they really never enjoy eternal life, which is now, because they continue to flirt with evil. Sin is still fascinating for them.

People who have denied themselves live at the pleasure of Christ. They realize that once the crowd dissipates and the show is over, all that will be left is Christ. One day Jesus performed one of His most notable miracles—He fed five thousand people at the Sea of Galilee. It was incredible due to the expense and the magnitude of the miracle. At that moment Christ's crowds swelled to an all-time high. People came to Jesus in droves. He was the Dude with the food. Everyone likes Jesus when He is the Dude with the food. You can just eat and eat and take and take and consume and consume until your heart is content. People love this one-dimensional Jesus.

Through the night Jesus sneaks over to the other side of the lake. The people start looking for the Dude with the food. They find Him across the lake and are ready for Him to do His next trick. To their surprise Jesus lays some hard truth down on them. "Jesus said to them, 'Very truly I tell you, unless you eat the flesh of the Son of Man and drink his blood, you have no life in you. Whoever eats my flesh and drinks my blood has eternal life, and I will raise them up at the last day. For my flesh is real food and my blood is real drink. Whoever eats my flesh and drinks my blood remains in me, and I in them. Just as the living Father sent me and I live because of the Father, so the one who feeds on me will live because of me.' . . . On hearing it, many of his disciples said, 'This is a hard teaching. Who can accept it?'" (John 6:53–57, 60, NIV).

Jesus drops the bomb on this crowd. He lets them know it is not just about bread and blessing; this is a lifestyle of self-denial. Jesus lived for the Father's glory, and He expects no less from His followers and fellow glory chasers. A. W. Tozer said, "Promoting self under the guise of promoting Christ is currently so common to excite little notice."[15] You know who does notice? Jesus.

When the smoke clears on this little gathering, the Bible says:

> Aware that his disciples were grumbling about this, Jesus said to them, "Does this offend you? Then what if you see the Son of Man ascend to where He was before! The Spirit gives life; the flesh counts for nothing. The words I have spoken to you—they are full of the Spirit and life. Yet there are some of you who do not believe." For Jesus had known from the beginning which of them did not believe and who would betray him. He went on to say, "This is why I told you that no one can come to me unless the Father has enabled them."
>
> From this time many of his disciples turned back and no longer followed Him.
>
> "You do not want to leave too, do you?" Jesus asked the Twelve.
>
> Simon Peter answered him, "Lord, to whom shall we go? You have the words of eternal life. We have come to believe and to know that you are the Holy One of God." (John 6:61–69, NIV)

When Jesus makes this statement, some of His closest friends, His twelve disciples, start grumbling. I imagine they thought, like many church leaders might today, *If He keeps saying things like that, He's going to run off our crowd.* While people mattered to Jesus, He never pandered to gather a crowd. Jesus never really cared about whom He offended with His words. In fact, the more religious you were then, and are now, the more you will be bruised by His words.

Finally, He looks at His disciples and asks them if they want to leave. Basically, He is asking them if they want to live for themselves. And Peter, the ignorant fisherman, says this: "Lord, to whom shall we go? You have the words of eternal life." People who have denied themselves know who has the words of life. Everyone has a place, a person, a source of where the words of life are found. Sold-out followers of Christ, glory chasers, know there is no other place to go. While the words may be hard, even painful, ultimately they give life. These men realized that living Christ's words meant denying their own logic and living for God's glory—the benefit of another.

Next Jesus demands that disciples take up a cross. This is a foreign concept for us. Someone once said, "One thing everyone knew about a man who was carrying his cross outside of town was that he was not coming back." The cross is arguably the cruelest instrument of death ever conceived in the depraved heart of man. The intent of the cross was for a person to hold on to life as long as possible and then die—to torture the flesh and then give it up in death. This is exactly what Christ calls us to do. Taking up our cross means publicly to identify with and suffer for Christ.

The apostle Paul said of himself: "I have been crucified with Christ. It is no longer I who live, but Christ who lives in me. And the life I now live in the flesh I live by faith in the Son of God, who loved me and gave himself for me" (Ga. 2:20). Paul had been an ambitious religious leader, a proud persecutor of the church. When he met Christ, all of his own ambition went away. He lived only and solely at Christ's directive.

Giving up our lives to the total control of God is tough—allowing Him to be responsible for the greatness or smallness of our lives. Letting God do things that seem to make no sense is hard. Just ask the Old Testament patriarch Abraham about this tension. You might remember that Abraham and his wife Sarah were given a son, Isaac, late in life. This boy was going to be the promise of an entire nation. Then, out of the blue, God asked Abraham to take his son, his only son, his pride and joy, his promised son to a mountain to sacrifice him. The Bible says of this event:

> Early the next morning Abraham got up and loaded his donkey. He took with him two of his servants and his son Isaac. When he had cut enough wood for the burnt offering, he set out for the place God had told him about. On the third day Abraham looked up and saw the place in the distance. He said to his servants, "Stay here with the donkey while I and the boy go over there. We will worship and then we will come back to you."
>
> Abraham took the wood for the burnt offering and placed it on his son Isaac, and he himself carried the fire and the knife. As the two of them went on together, Isaac spoke up and said to his father Abraham, "Father?"
>
> "Yes, my son?" Abraham replied.
>
> "The fire and wood are here," Isaac said, "but where is the lamb for the burnt offering?"
>
> Abraham answered, "God himself will provide the lamb for the burnt offering, my son." And the two of them went on together.
>
> When they reached the place God had told him about, Abraham built an altar there and arranged the wood on it. He bound his son Isaac and laid him on the altar, on top of the wood. Then he reached out his hand and took the knife to slay his son. But the angel of the Lord called out to him from heaven, "Abraham! Abraham!"
>
> "Here I am," he replied."
>
> Do not lay a hand on the boy," he said. "Do not do anything to him. Now I know that you fear God, because you have not withheld from me your son, your only son." (Gen. 22:3–12, NIV)

Can you imagine the conversation Abraham must have had with God the night before this event? I doubt he got much sleep. I bet Abraham was using every line of reasoning, every logical argument he could think of with God. This made no sense on any level. But ultimately Abraham got comfortable that his dream of having a son was about to die. He didn't know what God was doing, but he knew he was about to experience the greatest loss of this life. This boy had been given to him in his later years. He worshipped this boy, and that was the problem. The blessing of this young boy had become an idol to Abraham.

Now it's good the story doesn't end with the killing of young Isaac. And I doubt God will call any of you to kill your kids. In fact, if you are a kid reading this and your parents suggest taking you on a camping trip, like the one detailed above, call the local authorities. Taking up our crosses will mean killing some of our own dreams so that God's dream can live. Once Abraham crucified his own flesh, God was able to give him not only his son but also a nation. For more of God to live in us, more of us must die. This is not a one-and-done kind of thing. It is a daily dying.

Additionally Abraham suffered as a result of this decision with Isaac. We don't see in Scripture where Abraham ever lived with his wife, Sarah, again. The next time she is mentioned is when she died, "Sarah lived to be a hundred and twenty-seven years old. She died at Kiriath Arba (that is, Hebron) in the land of Canaan, and Abraham went to mourn for Sarah and to weep over her" (Gen. 23:1–2, NIV). It stands to reason that when Isaac gets home from the camping trip his mother might have a hard time with his attempted murder by his father. I imagine no matter how many times Abraham said, "God told me to do it!" it probably didn't jive with Momma Bear. When you follow Christ and pursue God's glory, some people won't get it. They will alienate you and estrange themselves from you. That is part of cross bearing.

Finally, Christ says to would-be followers, "Follow me." To follow Christ means to pursue His person. This pursuit will be persistent, ongoing, and never ending. As long as the disciple has breath in his body, he will be pursuing the Christ and the glory of God. And, as the disciple draws his first breath in eternity, it will only indicate a new beginning, without end, of knowing the vast glory of God forever.

Peter, one of the twelve disciples, is an interesting character in Christ's inner circle. Jesus began His relationship with Peter with these two simple words: "Follow me" (Mark 1:17). The first occasion was by the Sea of Galilee where Peter dropped his nets and began pursuing Christ. At that moment he had no idea of all the incredible things he would experience with that simple invitation. He had no idea that he was about to trade the rut of being a fisherman for walking on water. Pursuing Jesus brought with it the dangerous certainty of adventure far greater than he could have ever created in his own strength.

Do you think, if you were to follow Jesus with this type of relentless abandon, you could experience this kind of adventure? Can you imagine a life that is beyond your imagination? Christ followers, real disciples, have stories of the pursuit, the chasing of God's glory.

Later in Peter's life, just days before Christ would ascend to heaven, Jesus says again to him, "Follow me" (John 21:22). A lot of things have happened between these two callings. About halfway between the two, Peter realizes who Jesus is. He calls him the

"Christ" or "Messiah, the Son of the living God." Jesus commended Peter on this revelation because God, the Father, had revealed this to Peter. God knew Peter was chasing His glory and He could entrust more of Himself to Peter (Matt. 16:13–20). But right before this last "follow me," Peter told Jesus he would never deny Him. Christ predicted that Peter would deny Him three times. The prediction came true (Mark 14). Peter denies Christ and retreats back to the same lakeshore that Christ called him from the first time.

The risen Christ shows up on that seashore. He could have condemned Peter. He could have beat him up for his weakness. He could have totally disqualified Peter from having a part of any future ministry. Instead Jesus reinstates Peter into service. And this time Peter follows Christ in a new way—wholeheartedly. Peter will preach his first sermon under the power of the Holy Spirit, and thousands of people will respond. He will lead the first New Testament church, and the results of that are still felt today. He will go to his death for Jesus, being crucified upside down because he believed he wasn't worthy to die in the same manner Christ had died.

Following Jesus means relentlessly pursuing Him into the next adventure. It will be over your head. It will be scary. It will require strength greater than you can provide. It will be overwhelming, and it will be worth it. But remember, there is no glory in the expected.

Questions

1. Do you expect reward for you "good" behavior?

2. When have you had to surrender your will?

3. Where are you following Him today?

Chapter 7
Grow Up as Fast as You Can

Our present culture is experiencing some unique dynamics in young adult culture. Frankly it is taking each generation longer to grow up now than ever before. For instance, health-care legislation has the provision to allow children to remain on parental insurance until age twenty-six. I am all for people getting insurance, but this phenomena is radically contradictory to expectations for young adults less than one hundred years ago.

When my grandfather, Culas Rook, graduated from high school in the early 1940s, he had two options—go to war or go to work. Some people in his day went to college, but that was not the norm. He went to war, fought in the Philippines, and was out of the country for over four years without the luxuries of e-mail and cheap cellular services. While he was gone, some of his family died, others were born, but he was a man who acted like a man. Ironically, when he came back, he still acted like a man. He was married to one woman for four decades, was a great father, ran a business for fifty years, and every day he would take out that big old large-print Bible and read it and then go live it.

I believe the single biggest reason we have younger generations struggling to know *what to do* and *how to do* is due to our lack, as Christians and churches, of making disciples. I believe my grandfather's large-print Bible was the secret to his success.

I have an accountability buddy who gave me a rutu a few years ago. A rutu is a weapon the Maasai tribe in Africa give to their boys who are about to become men. Each young boy is given a rutu and a spear and then sent into the bush to stalk and kill a lion. If the boy kills the lion, he is now considered a man, but if the lion kills him, not so much. A clear rite of passage demonstrates when he has become a man. We lack, in our culture, rites of passage that demonstrate growth and adulthood. Since there is no clear path to adulthood, younger generations are spinning to know how to do the most basic of functions in life.

The bottom line is, without becoming a disciple, we cannot adequately articulate what it means to be a man or woman. Remember, God is all about His own glory. He is radically committed to Himself in all things. However, also remember that, while God is all about His own glory, He is about your good, and He knows what is the most good for you is His glory. So how do these two weighty realities work out in real life? How does being a disciple and God's glory work together?

Just before Jesus goes to the cross, He tells His disciples: "I am the vine; you are the branches. Whoever abides in me and I in him, he it is that bears much fruit, for apart from me you can do nothing. If anyone does not abide in me he is thrown away like a branch and withers; and the branches are gathered, thrown into the fire, and burned. If you abide in me, and my words abide in you, ask whatever you wish, and it will be done for you. By this my Father is glorified, that you bear much fruit and so prove to be my disciples" (John 15:5–8). God is glorified in the fruitfulness of our lives. I'll take it a step further: disciples are always fruitful. God cannot imagine a non-fruit-bearing Christian. If you are really a Christian, there must be some external evidence to this end, or you might simply be delusional. And here's the deal: if you are a Christian, you are by default a disciple. Apple trees grow apples. Orange trees grow oranges. You get the point. You are growing something. So what is it, and how do you know?

Many texts speak to disciple making, and many books have been written on this topic, but I am just a simple person. When you are not real smart, like me, you must be to the point. God wants us to know how we are doing. He wants us to experience the richness of His glory, and He wants to be glorified. I want you to see three stages of the discipleship process and some related characteristics. In 1 John 2:12–14, the Bible says: "I am writing to you, little children, because your sins are forgiven for his name's sake. I am writing to you, fathers, because you know him who is from the beginning. I am writing to you, young men, because you have overcome the evil one. I write to you, children, because you know the Father. I write to you, fathers, because you know him who is from the beginning. I write to you, young men, because you are strong, and the word of God abides in you, and you have overcome the evil one."

The text identifies three types of disciples—children, young men, and fathers. Ladies, do not be offended. This applies to you as well. As we examine each of these, begin to ask yourself, where am I in this journey?

Spiritual Children

When we had our son, it was a magical moment. I will never forget going to the doctor with my wife, Amy, one morning, thinking she was having false labor. Notice, I didn't say "we" were having false labor. I have never gone into labor in all of my life. I have never pushed out a kidney stone, much less a person. So, if you are a man reading this, you never have and never will go into labor.

I had been excited the entire pregnancy, eagerly anticipating the arrival of our son, Rook, named after my grandfather. She was in labor for many hours, and then he was finally taken by C-section. I will never forget his cone head. It was like a perfect arrow. His faintest cry brought me to attention. In a moment my life had been forever changed. I could not have imagined loving someone more so quickly.

Then, a few years later, we were blessed with the arrival of our little girl, Molly. For this birth I donned a pink T-shirt that said, "Tough Guys Wear Pink." I began to realize then and there that little girls will make dads do things they never thought they would. To this day Molly can talk me into things I never thought possible. Overnight my capacity to love increased again. I had wondered, when we found out we were having Molly, if my heart could really stretch, but when I saw that little girl, I was smitten.

Children are a great and indescribable blessing to any home, including the church. But children are the greatest problem in the home and the church, for that matter. Think about the lengths we go to ensure the safety of children.

The complexities of child protection begin before they ever make it home from the hospital. I remember having to show the hospital administration that I was competent to put the car seat in the car before we could take our son home. How ridiculous to make a grown man put a car seat in the car—the right way. And after I figured it out, with the help of a nurse, we got to take our child home. You would have thought by the time the second kid arrived I would have had the car seat deal down, but no. See, about every other year, baby manufacturers completely change baby accoutrements, so as to make parents look foolish and require the purchase of new gear—or so it seems.

Children require special food. It starts with milk or formula. They must be fed regularly or they get upset. They progress to soft foods. And then children just get picky, don't they? They start wanting certain foods. They will throw tantrums if they do not get what they want. Many a good restaurant experience has been ruined for their parents and others who had to hear the inconsolable screams of some little urchins that did not get what they wanted or got want they wanted and changed their mind.

Then, entire houses must be kid proofed for fear that children might kill themselves. Every cabinet and drawer must be made secure so the Ginsu knives you bought one night in a moment of weakness and insomnia don't hack little junior to the point of you taking him or her to the emergency room and you getting investigated by CPS. Baby gates are installed so the little bundle of joy doesn't bounce down the stairs. Electrical outlets are covered so the mini Thomas Edison doesn't stick a butter knife into the socket and discover the miracle of 110 volts the hard way.

Children are the pride of the home, without question, but they are the problem of the home as well. Kids naturally are self-centered and obsessed with their own needs. You do not have to teach a kid to be possessive. Children are born with an innate sense of possessiveness. They naturally take and steal from others. They want what they want. Their natural appetites are innately depraved. As children develop and grow, we naturally expect them to think about and respect the rights of others. It is imperative that they do not develop a God complex, believing that all the world is by and for them.

Vividly I can remember certain moments when my kids began to realize that others also happened to live on the planet. Sometimes it was the simple sharing of a toy with a friend or having to try some horrible-looking food item that was crammed into my face because they "made it." With each of these moments, as a parent, I was aware that their sense of others was growing. The same must be true in the church: spiritual kids must grow in their awareness of others.

And kids make a lot of messes, which parents and others must clean up. For instance, we expect them to poop themselves. While not a glamorous job in any way, shape, or form, adults clean children's backsides hundreds of times before they learn to take care of the basics of their God-given plumbing for themselves. While making a doodee, or any other name for one of the most foul things a body does to make it sound better, is acceptable for a one-year-old, it is completely unacceptable or cute when a kid is eighteen years old—providing the child has the ability to learn this necessary service.

I remember some of the nightmare blowouts of my children in the past. Fighting my own gag reflex, I would fight my way to their cribs, take the child to the changing table, and then proceed to clean up what only a parent or a billy goat would touch. If my children had not been potty trained in a reasonable amount of time, it would have been a reflection on me as a bad parent. The same is true for the spiritual nurture of spiritual children in the church. At some point, just like in the home, people need to grow up in the church.

Being a child is a stage in the discipleship process, just like being a child is a stage in physical maturity. The text gives two primary characteristics of people at this stage of the discipleship process—spiritual kids know their sins are forgiven, and they know the Father. They possess an elementary understanding of God. If you ask someone who has just trusted Christ as Savior what happened, they will most likely tell you they are not going to hell when they die because they have a relationship with the Father and they know that Jesus has forgiven their sins. They know the basics.

Every church ought to have a good number of spiritual kids. If a church lacks spiritual kids, something is wrong. Every church, if it is really a church, ought regularly to see the fruit of people coming to faith in Christ and knowing His Father. Jesus was clear that we are to "go and make disciples (Matt. 28:19–10); this is a nonnegotiable for the New Testament church. However, we need to have more of an expectation that spiritual children grow up in the church as fast as they can before these spiritual kids create problems.

Too many times churches allow a culture of immaturity. I would argue this is why we have big churches in the West with really shallow people. We propagate spiritual adolescence. Spiritual immaturity is evident in the lack of real conversion growth in most churches. Few churches will baptize more than one hundred people in a given year; yet some of these same churches will experience "growth." Why? Because the spiritual children of one church down the street got upset because some program they wanted was taken away—not realizing what they really needed was presence. Some expectation of theirs was not pacified—the wrong music, not a hip enough kids' ministry. They didn't feel something they were looking for—some type of holy buzz. Maybe they were no longer coddled by the pastor. These children wanted to continue to drink milk and not move on to food. Therefore, they took their toys and went down the street.

But I suspect that much spiritual immaturity found in most churches is due to pastors and leaders who have not clearly marked the path of discipleship for their members. It is hard to become what you have never been shown. The sad reality is that many churches have spiritual kids who are now in their forties, fifties, sixties, and beyond because the church has allowed generations of spiritual babies who can now shave their faces and their legs but still know only elementary truths about their sins and the Father.

People who stay at this level live a selfish Christianity. They continue to live carnal, worldly lives, seeking their own desires. Sadly they live with a false understanding of forgiveness and the Father. Typically they function out of one of two extremes—either incredible license to do whatever they want to do or intense legalism where they live joyless, law-bound lives.

A number of years ago, I had a couple of self-professed Christ followers ask me to marry them. Upon my interview I realized they were living together. I asked if they knew this was contrary to what the Bible taught about how we are to marry. They both indicated, with a bashful look, that they knew this was not God's way. They wanted this big, elaborate wedding to share with their friends and family. I wanted them to experience God's best for their marriage. I gave them two options. First, I could marry them in my office within the next week. They could repent and immediately seek to set things right. Therefore, making their relationship blessable. Second, they could move apart, seek biblical counseling, and determine if this is really what God intended for them. In the interim I offered to help find the man a temporary living arrangement to offset his expenses while they sought the Lord.

We got back together a few days later so I could hear what they decided. The young man looked at me and asked if he could ask me a question. I could tell this was going to be a good one so I played along. He asked, "Doesn't God forgive all sin?"

I said, "Sure."

And he continued, "Well, we are going to continue to live together, and right before we get married, we are going to ask God to forgive us because He has to forgive us if we ask."

I shook my head in disbelief. I couldn't believe the audacity I was hearing. Yet, to their defense, this was the God that "church" had taught them. I said, "God is not under any obligation to forgive your premeditated sin. God only forgives repentant people, and that is not repentance—you want convenience." I tried to leave the door open to this couple to grow up, but it was to no avail. Unfortunately, I never heard from them again. This example is representative of spiritual immaturity in the church today. God is a means to my end. Spiritual children will think this way unless they are forced to grow up.

Another extreme traps spiritual children—legalism. It reminds me of growing up in my home church where everyone was given an envelope with a bunch of boxes to check off weekly. The boxes were things like "brought your Bible," "read your Bible daily," "brought an offering," and "witnessing." Everyone pretty much lied on the last one. For many the Father was about checking some boxes. My sins were forgiven, and the Father doesn't want me to mess up, so I ensure I don't mess up by checking these boxes, making me acceptable to Him. Now there is no joy or happiness in this, but I am duty bound. Duty-bound Christianity might look more impressive, but there is no real desire to know the Father, just to get the benefits from Him—mainly my sins are forgiven.

Churches are full of this type of Christian, people who simply use the Father to get what they want. The sad reality is, in the examples mentioned above, they might not even know the Father. Remember, disciples display fruit for the glory of God. Without fruit there is no proof of profession. It is possible to know about the Father and not know Him personally.

Spiritual Young Men

The next stage of discipleship is that of a spiritual young man or woman. Let me stress that your chronological age and your spiritual age are in no way or shape connected. There are three notable characteristics of people at this age—they are strong, the Word of God abides in them, and they have overcome the evil one.

Before we dive into the particular characteristics, notice that the text jumps from spiritual children to young men. Note young men, not young adolescents. There is correlation to spiritual maturity and practical maturity. You show me a truly mature Christian young man, and I will show you a practically mature adult. Understand we have created this thing called adolescence in the culture. Adolescence is not a biblical concept. Adolescence is a man-made invention intended to prolong the dangers of immaturity. It is dangerous for kids to remain kids. You are more susceptible to danger and injury as a child. Young adults have always paved the way for culture. From the book *Do Hard Things* consider these revelations.

- A young lady, Clarissa, at only eleven years of age began caring for her first patient, her brother David, after he fell from a rafter in their unfinished barn. Clara stayed at his side for three years and learned to administer all his medicines, including the "great, loathsome crawling leeches."

- At age seventeen a young man named George, back in 1749, was appointed official surveyor for Culpeper County, Virginia, a well-paid position which enabled him to purchase land in the Shenandoah Valley, the first of his many land acquisitions in Western Virginia.

- David, at the young age of nine, through the influence of his adoptive father, was commissioned a midshipman in the United States Navy in 1810. Three years later, when he was only twelve years of age, David was given command of a captured enemy ship and brought her safely to port.

On April 21, 1861, nine days after the start of the Civil War, Clarissa, who had doctored her brother David, tended to wounded Massachusetts soldiers quartered in the United States Senate chamber in Washington. After the First Battle of Bull Run, July 21, she established the main agency to obtain and distribute supplies to wounded soldiers. She was given a pass to ride in army ambulances to provide comfort to the soldiers and nurse them back to health. Today we remember her as Clara Barton, the founder of the American Red Cross.

Young George went on to become the dominant military and political leader of the new United States of America from 1775 to 1799, known as the "father of our country," George Washington, the first president of the United States of America.

A prize master by the age of twelve, David was promoted to lieutenant in 1822, commander in 1844, and captain in 1855. In 1866, after the American Civil War, David Farragut became the first admiral of the United States Navy.[16]

Scripture says, "Let no one despise you for your youth, but set the believers an example in speech, in conduct, in love, in faith, in purity" (1 Tim. 4:12). Age is not an excuse for immaturity. When people come to faith in Christ, it is imperative that they grow up—and fast. Immaturity is a waste of time for your own good and God's glory.

The first characteristic of spiritual young men is that they are strong. This speaks of physical and spiritual stature—they are healthy. Young men are in the prime of their life. Now what makes a young man a young man? He has gone through puberty. His voice changes. His complexion does crazy things. His body matures to the point that He can reproduce himself. This ability for a man to reproduce himself makes him a man. So this spiritual young man is strong because he can reproduce the gospel in other people. In other words, he can lead someone to faith in Christ.

I will never forget the way I was trained to lead people to Christ. My friend Chad, who is now a missionary, took me as an eighth-grader to the bowling alley in our town. Before we arrived, he gave me a crash course on how to share Christ with people. At the beginning of our evening, he said, "If you don't share your faith with someone in this bowling alley, you are going to need to call your mother to come and pick you up." He was serious. I was going home with Mommy if I didn't grow up. Some might dispute the tactic, but it worked—I grew up that night. I wish I could report someone came to know Christ, but they didn't. I realized though, as an eighth-grader, that I could share the gospel.

Another characteristic of a young man is that the Word abides in him. Let me be frank—if you can't figure out how to read and study your Bible on your own, you will remain a spiritual baby messing your proverbial spiritual drawers. The text says to "abide in my word" (John 8:31). The meaning of *abide* is simply "to remain." These spiritual young men stay connected to the Word, the Bible, and the Word works in them. Did you catch that? The Word works. When you abide, the Word changes you from the inside out.

The method you use to get the Bible into your life can vary from person to person. Some people can just read the Bible straight through. Others need a reading plan. I know some people who listen to the Bible on their daily commutes. The point is, get the word in you.

The final characteristic of young men is that they overcome the evil one. It is important to know that a Christian has three primary adversaries that all find their origin in Satan, the evil one. The first is the world. The world system is a fallen, broken system. In the world system many times evil is protected, and just people are punished. This should be of no surprise. Then there is the flesh within each believer, those unregenerated parts of us that we do not give over to the Lord. It might be an addiction, an attitude, or an activity. This side of eternity there will always be parts of ourselves that need to be yielded to God. And, finally, there is Satan himself, that the believer could do battle with. Let me correct something at this point. Satan is not omnipresent, meaning "everywhere," or omniscient, meaning "all knowing," or omnipotent, meaning "all powerful." He is limited in his abilities. A defeated foe, his destiny is the lake of fire or hell. He will be there with other people who have chased their own glory. Given his limited abilities, I doubt too many of us will face Satan head-on. He practically has bigger fish to fry than most of us. He does, however, have demons that work to do his bidding so the demonic is absolutely true and needs to be considered at all times.

Practicly spiritual young men are disciples who are overcoming the evil one and are having more days of victory over their sin and selfishness than not. There is a general lessening of worldly things. They are not enamored with the best this world can offer. They know they were created for something and someone bigger. They are regularly, daily crucifying the unregenerated parts of themselves to the cross (1 Cor. 15:31), knowing that only the cross can kill off the evil that lives still in the members of their body. And they do not look to fight the devil, but they stand their ground when confronted with the demonic. They have victory in their faith.

The church today is crying out for some believers to grow up in their faith, to become young adults—regardless of their chronology—to step up. The church is dying because of its juvenile tendencies. Grow up!

Spiritual Fathers

This text gives the summit of all activity for the Christian, the disciple. It is to know the Father. This is the only characteristic of a father. Think about it. The spiritual mother or father has all the characteristics of the spiritual young man but has reached the zenith, knowing the Father.

Young men are ambitious. There is nothing wrong with ambition when it is tempered by God's Spirit. But young men can become argumentative. Young men are the ones who cover their bodies in paint and cheer wildly for their sporting teams every week during football season. They want to compete and win. They want their team to win. They can easily go off on tangents.

This is true of spiritual young men. I must admit—I love to win. I love success. The church can be a great place for me to hide out. This is the area of my shortfall. If you are "successful" in the church world by having more bodies, buildings, and bucks, people will not only applaud your efforts but reward them. They will let you speak at conferences, buy your books, and give weight to your words. Many people are regarded in the church today who are not really spiritual fathers but who are treated as such due to their apparent successes.

Spiritual fathers have the genuine characteristic that they know the Father and He is enough. The word *know* does not mean to know intellectually; it means "to know God experientially, intimately." These disciples have come to the point where they know the only thing that matters is not a thing, an outcome, a position but a person, the Father. For these the Father is their portion. When God divided the promised land to the people of Israel, He gave all the twelve tribes of Israel land but one—the Levites. Of the Levites the Bible says: "And the Lord said to Aaron, 'You shall have no inheritance in their land, neither shall you have any portion among them. I am your portion and your inheritance among the people of Israel'" (Num. 18:20). God Himself was going to be enough for the Levites—and for you, if you long to be a spiritual father. The Father becomes our prize. As A. W. Tozer says, "The man who has God for his treasure has all things in One."[17]

Paul, the apostle, said it like this: "Indeed, I count everything as loss because of the surpassing worth of knowing Christ Jesus my Lord. For his sake I have suffered the loss of all things and count them as rubbish, in order that I may gain Christ" (Phil. 3:8). If you can know God, what else is worth your time, energy, investment? Nothing! Spiritual fathers get it. Do you?

When this is all said and done, when your life is over, when everything is finished, what will be your greatest boast? It is important to know what you are striving for—what success will look like for you. Will you take the great challenge of our day to grow up? In a culture of immaturity, will you become a disciple? Will you know the Father? Everything else is a waste of your time and greatest efforts.

Questions

1. Where are you in the growth process?
2. What is your greatest hindrance to growth?
3. What is the boast of your life?

Chapter 8
Superpowers

I have wished I had superpowers ever since I was a kid. Back in the day the greatest thing ever invented for kids with overactive imaginations was Underoos. Underoos were underwear that immediately turned you from the mild-mannered Clark Kent into Superman or from Bruce Wayne into Batman. Immediately after bursting through the door from elementary school, the clothes came off and the Underoos came out—I was a superhero—at least until dinner.

In my teen years I wanted other superpowers like the ability of retaining information necessary for tests without studying. Or the power to make zits disappear on command. There were times I wished for superpowers to make girls like me. I thought it would be cool to be like a Jedi Knight and simply wave my hand in front of a girl's face and say, "This is the boy you are looking for. Date him." Unfortunately the kryptonite of my body odor often debunked this power.

As I got older, I began to wish for the ability to shoot lasers out of my fingers to eradicate slow-moving vehicles who were always in my lane of traffic. I also wanted the ability to change the bad breath of people who always wanted to tell me secrets and talk really, really close.

Later in life I have wanted the superpower to regrow hair. I don't know who coined the phrase "male-pattern baldness," but I have been looking for years, and I still see no pattern. I have also wanted the powers of Stretch Armstrong to make me taller, but I guess I will have to settle for Dr. Scholls' shoe lifts.

Even today I am a sucker for a superhero movie, and I guess a whole bunch of other people are too because they continue to make movies each year like Ironman, X-Men, Star Wars, Superman, Thor, and the like. With each release sales continue to break box-office records.

The truth is, I know for me, and I suppose for others, I just want to have some normal powers. I just want to be married to the same woman for my lifetime. I love my wife, Amy. She is awesome. We have known each other since we were kids. We have been married for nearly twenty years. I don't ever want to hurt her in any way. But I constantly see, hear, and have to help people pick up the pieces of marriages that have busted apart. Marriage is and was God's basic unit of stability not just for us as individuals but for us as a culture. We, all of us in the world, have a hard time getting married, which is obvious because cohabitation is at an epic number, and staying married because a ridiculous number of marriages end in divorce. It is apparent we need some kind of superpower to help us.

I love my kids, Rook and Molly. They are the greatest blessings of my life. I want to be the dad they need. Here is the deal—raising kids is hard. All the people with kids reading this, back me up! There are no manuals for raising kids, and every kid is different. Frankly we are less equipped and trained, generally, to raise kids than to drive a car. At least to drive a car you must go to driver's ed. Anybody with properly functioning reproductive equipment can have a child. But having a child and being a parent—a dad or a mom—requires superpowers.

I'm a pastor. Many pastors, for whatever reasons, never finish their ministries. Somewhere along the way by means of a stupid moral or financial decision, they have disqualified themselves. Or, after the long-term discouragement of leading ungrateful, demanding, and, in some cases, downright demon-spawned church members, they quit. Then there are the unseen spiritual forces of darkness that consistently pound on ministers, causing them to give up. As I have considered these things for my own life, one thing is certain: I need some sort of superpower.

Throughout history and the pages of the Bible, Christ followers have always had superpowers. I mean, these ordinary, oftentimes weak, most of the time self-conscious people were used by God to do incredible things, things beyond their own natural capacities.

Christians have done the hard things in each generation. Christians ran into Roman cities when plagues gripped major metropolitan areas to serve and save the dying and ill with no regard for their own safety. Christians have taken care of children all over the world at their own time and expense. Just consider the work of the George W. Bush administration that, because of biblical principles, spent time and money to help the AIDS epidemic in Africa. Christians have lobbied to end cruel institutions such as slavery and human trafficking. Just consider the ministry of John Newton, the mentor of William Wilberforce, who, through the power of the cross, sought to emancipate his fellowman. Christians have stood up to tyrannical kings and dictators at the expense of their own lives and hardship on their own families. Consider the life of Martin Luther, the great Reformer, who would not recant what the Scriptures clearly taught and believed that if his death was needed, then death would be better than blasphemy. Think of Dietrich Bonhoeffer, the great German Baptist pastor who plotted the assassination of Adolf Hitler, only to be executed for treason just days before the Allied liberation of Germany. And in our time, consider the faceless masses of the martyrs who have paid the price for their faith in their own blood. More people died for the faith in the twentieth century than in any other time in history. My friend from Africa witnessed his own brother's martyrdom when he was thrown into a wood chipper and his remains blown into a raging river. In light of all of these, is your faith advancing?

So, what hope do we have in trying to live the Christian life? How do we grow up? I mean, surely there's got to be a way for us to accomplish and do what God has clearly called us to do. When Jesus left the planet, He told His disciples that He would send to them the Holy Spirit, the Superpower. The Holy Spirit, or the Paraclete, means "the helper." Jesus had to leave the planet so the Holy Spirit could arrive to empower people like us. The best part about the Holy Spirit was that He wasn't going to live near us, or around this, or above us, but inside us. John 14:15–17 says: "If you love me, you will keep my commandments. And I will ask the Father, and he will give you another Helper, to be with you forever, even the Spirit of truth, whom the world cannot receive, because it neither sees him nor knows him. You know him, for he dwells with you and will be in you."

Did you catch that? You cannot live the Christian life in your own strength because you do not have superpowers within yourself. It simply cannot be done. Christ followers in all generations cannot live the Christian life in their own strength. They will constantly revert back to their own sin, selfishness, and fears if they try to live apart from the Holy Spirit, the Superpower.

In attempting to live the Christian life, many of us struggle with is our own determination. We do not like being dependent on anyone or anything. As children we work hard to gain our independence. Then, as adults, we work hard to try to retain our independence. Let me demonstrate: children are constantly trying to grow and get access to greater opportunity—to stay up later, get more responsibility, and the like. Senior adults are trying to stay out of nursing homes and assisted living centers to keep their independence. They do not want to be told when to eat, sleep, and deal with their bodily issues. You dig? Dependency is something we resist at great lengths. But dependency is the only way you can be a Christ follower, for we are incapable of living the Christian life in our own strength. We need the superpower of the Holy Spirit.

When I was young, I heard few sermons preached on the power of the Holy Spirit. In my evangelical flavor we treated the Holy Spirit like our crazy uncle at the family reunion. We all have crazy people in our families. We just don't like to admit it. For instance, I went to my family reunion, and this one family member had a barbecue pit welded to the back bumper of his car. As he pulled into the state park where we were assembling, everyone noticed that his car was smoking a lot. When he got out of the car, a few sheets in the wind I might add, we immediately asked if he and his vehicle were OK. He assured us that he and his fine automobile were marvelous and took us to the rear of the vehicle where he showed us his aftermarket addition of a barbecue grill welded to his back bumper, next to the gas tank. You can't make up this kind of story; you have to be related to it. He opened his mobile grilling mechanism and to our delight showed us the brisket he intended the family to dine on that afternoon that, having cooked it on the trip up. That is what I call multitasking.

For fear of what people might think, many have failed to recognize God's plan of dependency found only in the person and the work of the Holy Spirit in their lives. The Holy Spirit will make you uncomfortable. The Holy Spirit will interrupt you at the most inopportune times. Until we embrace this understanding of the Holy Spirit, you and I will be incapable of living the Christian life. The Holy Spirit gives us the ability to live bigger than ourselves. Notice the words of Ephesians 5:17–21: "Therefore do not be foolish, but understand what the will of the Lord is. And do not get drunk with wine, for that is debauchery, but be filled with the Spirit, addressing one another in psalms and hymns and spiritual songs, singing and making melody to the Lord with your heart, giving thanks always and for everything to God the father in the name of our Lord Jesus Christ."

One of the best parts of the Holy Spirit is His role in helping us find and understand God's will. Over the years I have heard many people ask a question like this, "What is God's will for me?" Now that doesn't sound like a bad question, does it? I mean, who would not want to know what God's will or plan is for their life. The trouble with this question is the subject of the question—*me*. Many people want to know God's will only as it pertains to them. God is working out His will in everyone's life. If we could see things from His vantage point, we would recognize there is really only one will—*His*. First Corinthians 2:10 says, "These things God has revealed to us through the Spirit. For the Spirit searches everything, even the depths of God." God is using His Spirit to bring out His will in all people and in all times. So really there is just God's will. A better question might be, how can I get my life in the center of God's will?

This is where the Holy Spirit is invaluable to us; this is where we are dependent on the Spirit.

The Ephesians text says, "Do not get drunk with wine, . . . but be filled with the Spirit." I've always found great irony in the wordplay between drunkenness, mentioned here, and the Holy Spirit. People got drunk on spirits in Jesus' day and still do in our day. While I would never in any way promote drunkenness, I will say it has provided some rather interesting YouTube videos. People who get drunk typically lose their natural abilities to function. They may slur their speech or use different words. They may not be able to walk in a straight line. Things they typically would know, they don't know anymore. And so it is with people who walk according to the superpower of the Holy Spirit. Paul said it like this in 2 Corinthians 5:13 (NIV), "If we are 'out of our mind,' as some say, it is for God; if we are in our right mind, it is for you." "If we are 'out of our mind'"—what a great line. The Holy Spirit will cause you to do something you would have never done in your own power. The Holy Spirit will lead, guide, and direct you in ways that will and should seem funny to people who do not have the Superpower you possess.

It seems like with each passing year at the church I serve, we send more people around the world to tell others about Jesus. Hundreds of people sacrifice their money, time, and other opportunities to share the truth about Jesus with complete strangers they will never meet again. Why? Because this crazy, wonderful power of the Holy Spirit resides in them. I can't explain it, but I have prayed for and with people doctors had given up hope of finding a cure for their illnesses and diseases, only to have them make full recoveries. How? The power of the Holy Spirit. Every year marriages that should have ended in divorce get put back together. Why? The supernatural power of the Holy Spirit. I remember having a couple tell me about a sordid affair the wife was having, and within months that couple was disciplining other couples. Do you get it? The Holy Spirit is not just a thing in the Christian's life; He is *the* thing. This wild and wonderful Superpower, the Holy Spirit, is the secret to putting life all together for each of us Christ followers.

Notice what this text says about a change in behavior we possess under this Superpower. First, He changes our language. Ephesians says, "Addressing one another in psalms and hymns." The Spirit has a direct effect on our language. Have you ever known anybody who had an uncontrollable mouth? Maybe they are the chronic gossip, the one who always knows the latest story. Maybe it's the person who's overly critical and never has a kind word to say to anyone. Like most narcissists, it's the constant self-promotion that spews out of that neighbor's or family member's or coworker's mouth. Maybe you're the guy in this coffee shop where I am writing this who continues to curse his laptop to the chagrin of those of us around him. Maybe it's you. Perhaps you have felt like giving up because you can't do it—you can't change what comes out of your mouth. And here's the deal, you're right—you cannot do it. Your only chance is to yield your tongue to the Spirit's power.

But it gets better, especially for dented cans like us. The text says, "Singing and making melody to the Lord with your heart." The Holy Spirit gives you the power to stay God focused and tethered to His heart. In our own strength we have the tendency to wander away from God. We are like animals who do not know we have a benevolent master. I'm not a big animal guy. But I do live with some animals. In particular we have this dog named Swanson. Swanson is an English cavalier spaniel, black-and-white mix. Swanson has everything a dog could possibly want: he's well fed, well groomed, and he sleeps in a place far greater than his need—the laundry room. But Swanson has a peculiar tendency. Anytime the front door is left open, he immediately runs into the street. Not looking or not realizing the dangers, he runs for it. Somehow my misguided canine thinks he is best served being out of the presence of his master. What normally happens is one of his masters chases him down and brings him back home. I hope one day that dog figures out that we have his best interests in mind.

      Like Swanson we have a tendency to wander away from our Master. The best part is the Holy Spirit, our Superpower, does not have to chase us down, if He really does live in us, because He is already there. The Holy Spirit allows us to worship God in the throne room of our heart without interruption and remain tethered to Him at all times. And this is why we can sing and make melody to the Lord with our heart, not due to our willpower but because of this greater reality living inside us keeping us connected to Him.

      Check this out: the text goes on to say, "Giving thanks always and for everything to God the Father in the name of the Lord Jesus Christ." It is easy for us to live discontented lives. To always be looking at what others have and what I do not have. We covet the blessings of other people and fail to remember how highly we've been regarded by God. Sometimes, as a pastor, I have to admit that I really like the fruit I see in someone else's ministry. I think to myself, *I wonder why God has not given that to me?* I am sure you have never felt this way, but I have. I have thought to myself, *I am better at this or that than that person. Why are they so blessed?* Left to my narcissistic tendencies, I will be eaten up with envy and discontentment every time. What about you? The Superpower, the Holy Spirit, enables you and me to be grateful, fighting back the chronic fatigue of discontentment that regularly bombards us in the culture in which we live.

Think about it. You are intentionally targeted from the time you get up in the mornings until the time you go to bed each night with thousands of messages of discontentment. Constantly we are told we need something new to replace the something we bought last year. I remember once as a child my family was going through hard financial times. My father had lost his job. My parents were doing all they could for our family to make it. I knew that everything my parents did was out of sacrifice. It was time for school to start, and my mom took me to Kmart to buy school clothes. I had never bought clothes at Kmart. Knowing the pressure my parents were under, I was so grateful for every piece of clothing my mother bought me. Every piece of clothing was an incredible blessing. A few years later things changed. My parents' economic fortune had changed. My mother took me to buy school clothes once again. We went to name-brand stores to buy name-brand clothing. As the day progressed, I continued to complain about each article of clothing my mom suggested. It might have been the angst of being a preteen, but it was most likely a lack of allowing the Holy Spirit to work in me. Finally, in complete exhaustion my mother said, "You were sure more grateful when we shopped at Kmart. What happened?" What happened was I simply became discontented. Discontentment is the natural default of every person. Only with the superpower of the Holy Spirit can we be grateful people. What about you? Do you always have to have the fastest car? Do you always have to upgrade to the latest technology? Can you wear clothes for utility and not status? Only the Holy Spirit brings contentment.

The real kicker is found at the end of this little text where we are told, "Submitting to one another out of reverence for Christ." In the text that follows, wives are told to submit to husbands, children are told to submit to parents, and slaves are told to submit to masters. Narcissistic people do not like being told what to do. And in the day and age in which we live, everyone is empowered. It doesn't matter your gender, sexual orientation, status, or state of life, you are empowered to be and should not be told by anyone what to do. The trouble with this is, not everyone can be the boss. God has always given us a structure called "authority" by which we are to live. However, since the garden, He has known we are rebellious people who would not be willing to submit to anyone. Therefore, He, through the Spirit, causes us to do what we cannot do in our own strength. We are rebellious people who do not have the natural capacity to submit.

God has always had a plan from the beginning for narcissistic people like you and me—a plan that depends solely on Him to do what we cannot do. Now, as we will see going forward, this is not an excuse for us to be lazy in our spirituality. We are just reminded that we cannot do this on our own—in any way, shape, or fashion. God has had a plan from the beginning that we would be dependent on Him for everything. Back in the garden of Eden, God intended for Adam and Eve to depend on Him. And He intends for you and me to depend solely on Him for everything today.

Making It Real

So, how do we practically do this? I mean, we all know that the Holy Spirit is available to us, but how do we practically access this potent power? Ephesians 1:13 says, "In him you also, when you heard the word of truth, the gospel of your salvation, and believed in him, were sealed with the promised Holy Spirit." First, you must believe the Holy Spirit lives in you. When you trusted Christ as your Savior and Lord, the Holy Spirit took residence in you. The power that raised Jesus from the grave animates you.

Then you must appropriate the power that is within you. Galatians 3:3 says, "Are you so foolish? Having begun by the Spirit, are you now being perfected by the flesh?" You must ask the Holy Spirit to fill you regularly. When you feel you can't do it, that is indication that you do not have the ability to accomplish what only the Holy Spirit can in you. Daily, before I get out of bed and my feet touch the floor, I ask the Holy Spirit to fill me. My prayer each morning sounds like this, "Holy Spirit, I do not know what is going to happen today, but I know with Your power I can face anything. I invite You into this day. Interrupt me along the way so I can be fully used by You." I meet many believers who get overwhelmed by life and do not acknowledge the power that is within them.

Finally, you must believe the Holy Spirit is really within you. The Father has not left you to live the Christian life on your own. He gives you His Spirit so He can get the glory from your life. Romans 5:5 says, "And hope does not put us to shame, because God's love has been poured into our hearts through the Holy Spirit who has been given to us." You can deal with whatever is in front of you because of what the Holy Spirit does in you. Never underestimate the Spirit.

Questions

1. How familiar are you with the Holy Spirit?
2. What is the last thing the Holy Spirit led you to do?
3. What are you dependent on other than the Holy Spirit?

Chapter 9
The Final Warning: The Scariest Story in the Bible

How do you convince people that an incredibly beautiful blue lagoon is actually toxic? This was the problem of the town of Buxton, England. The town had a beautiful blue lagoon, which attracted people from far and near to go for a swim. Despite its charm, what lurked in the waters was potentially fatal. The lagoon had a pH level of 11.3, which means nothing until you consider that ammonia has a pH of 11.5 and bleach has a pH of 12.6. The high pH levels could cause skin and eye irritations, stomach problems, and fungal infections. To be honest it sounds like most community pools. To make matters worse, the lagoon was polluted. Warning signs posted such as, "Warning! Polluted water lagoon known to contain: car wrecks, dead animals, excrement, rubbish." Ironically, this was not enough to keep outdoor enthusiasts from swimming in the nasty waters. The deceptive looks of this lagoon drew people into these waters of death. Can you imagine swimming in excrement, trash, and animal carcasses—all the while your eyes are burning? The town eventually dyed the lagoon black, making it look like what it really was—toxic. The warnings simply did not work.[18]

A brand of Christianity is being propagated that is fatal. It looks good externally. It will be blessed culturally. It might even give a measure of comfort to its practitioners, but it does not end well at all. When we truly understand the awesomeness of living solely for the glory of God in all things, every other thing about our lives is altered. God has placed eternity in our hearts (Eccl. 3:11), and to pursue something other than the eternal results minimally in our boredom and possibly in our eternal destruction. When a Christian complains about being bored, it is a sure sign of living for lesser things. They try this and that to fill the space only eternity can fill. If you are a Christ follower, you must live for eternity, which begins now.

The Setup

Scripture tells a chilling story about a man who is classically called the rich, young ruler—a glory chaser. All Gospels except the Gospel of John contain this story, each one giving more and more detail about the young man. Let's set the stage. Many of the characteristics that describe this man are true for many twenty-first-century church attenders.

First, this man was rich (Luke 18:23). There is nothing wrong with wealth as long has you have attained it through biblical and legal means. If you can be wealthy, great. I bet most poor people would change spots with you in a heartbeat. I put this out there because most of you reading this are rich by global standards. If you have food in the cabinet and another change of clothes in your closet, you are loaded. You might not be rich compared to your neighbors, your family, or even the church parking lot, but you are loaded. If you really want to understand how wealthy you are, check out www.globalrichlist.com. It will open your eyes to your own reality.

Next we find out that this man was young (Matt. 19:22). Being young is awesome. When you are young, all of your parts work when they are supposed to work. The world is in front of you, and nothing seems unconquerable. Spiritually speaking, youth is not an excuse for stupidity, laziness, or wandering. Paul says to his young friend, "Let no one despise you for your youth, but set the believers an example in speech, in conduct, in love, in faith, in purity" (1 Tim. 4:12). This young man was bright and had a tremendous future in front of him. If you are reading this, you are either young, or you can be young in heart. I have known eighty-year-olds who are vibrant and full of life, and I have known forty-year-olds who died in their twenties but haven't lain down in actual death yet. So this applies to you.

Last, the young man was a ruler (Luke 18:18). He was a leader in the local synagogue, or he might have even been part of the ruling body of the Jewish Sanhedrin. Either way, he was a respected religious leader. He was widely and publicly recognized for his faith. More than just a "church attender," he was leading the charge. He was a point man. I suspect that many people reading this are part of a church; you might even have a leadership role in some way, shape, or form.

Here's the deal: if this guy showed up one Sunday in most churches in America, looking for a new church home, we would not only welcome him with open arms; I imagine many churches would promote this guy into leadership quickly. Before you know it, he would be leading this ministry or heading up this small group. What is not to like about this guy? We love this type of person in most churches. Who wouldn't? But, like toxic lagoons, looks can be deceiving.

The Barrier of Religion

In Luke's account the Bible says this ruler asked him, "'Good Teacher, what must I do to inherit eternal life?' And Jesus said to him, 'Why do you call me good? No one is good except God alone. You know the commandments: "Do not commit adultery, Do not murder, Do not steal, Do not bear false witness, Honor your father and mother."' And he said, 'All these I have kept from my youth'" (Luke 18:21–22).

This rich, young ruler was searching. The religion he had known to this point did not fill the deep longing of his heart. Religion is always man's attempt to manage God and make God more in man's own image. It is spiritual OCD (obsessive-compulsive disorder). We construct ritual and structure to try to put God in our service. Religion tries to exploit God for what He can do for us. God hates religion. This man had obviously had enough religion. He ran and bowed before Jesus; he bowed in front of a crowd of people. Leaders did not typically stoop, especially to someone who might be considered inferior in status like this preacher-carpenter, Jesus. Yet his posture indicates he was sincere.

Sincerity means "to be genuine." Yet sincerity is not the same thing as humility. Humility is not thinking less of yourself; it is just not thinking about yourself at all. You can be sincere and still be prideful. God only gives grace, His unmerited favor, to the humble, not the sincere. A lot of sincere people won't make it into heaven. The demons of hell sincerely believe in God, and they even shutter (James 2:19). Religion, sincere religion, is still religion.

But the trap of religion was obviously damning to this young man because he asked, "What must I do to inherit eternal life?" He thought salvation could be earned through religious exercise.

He felt he was capable in his own power and resources to merit eternal life. Religion will always make us feel better about ourselves because all we have to do is religious activities. It compares us to others and not to the standard of Christ.

Jesus is so patient with this religious poser, not wanting him to remain a religious weasel. He first asks the rich, young ruler, "Why do you call me good? No one is good except God alone." Jesus was not refuting the fact He was good or that He was God. Jesus just wanted to see if the man was putting all of this together. God was standing before him. People infected by religion can't discern if God is truly in their midst. Their own ideas, customs, and rules about God make it difficult for them to see God for who He really is.

It was like when my kids were really little, like two or three years old. I would play hide-and-seek with them. I would tell them to count to ten and then come and find me. I would hide in obvious places, basically out in the open, making it easy for them to find me. Yet many times they would just walk by me, not noticing me at all. They had in their minds some place they thought I might be and were not open to where I really was, which was in front of them. This man was so steeped in religion that he missed God in his midst. You think this happens today?

Jesus then followed up with another statement about keeping the commandments—no adultery, no murder, honoring parents, etc. The man assures Jesus that he has kept these commandments his entire life. What Jesus does here is genius. Jesus intentionally tests this young man on the commands that deal will outward religion. The answer to these commands is either yes or no. They are external works of religion. Many people can pass this test—the religion test.

I find that people who are caught in religion are typically quick to spout off their spiritual resume, much like this guy. Sometimes I will ask someone the question, "How are you doing spiritually?" Many times I get a list of accomplishments like, "Well, I am tithing, if that is what you mean, Preacher." Or, "I volunteer in the preschool ministry." Or, "I work in the parking lot on Sundays." While those activities are good and could indicate a growing relationship with God, they are not the guarantees of relational intimacy.

If you want to cut to the chase with people about God, ask them how their relationship with God is. If they start giving you the details of what they do—like give money, or serve, or do this or that, they might not have a relationship with God; they might be trapped in religion. If you ask me, "Kris, how is your relationship with your wife?" I will not tell you, "I took out the trash, I bought her flowers, and I did this and that." No, I will tell you about the quality of the relationship. I will give you relational details. I might say, "Amy and I are really connecting in the area of communication." Or I might say, "We are having to make sure we are prioritizing time for each other." The same is true with Christ. Relationships are dynamic, not static. Christ followers use relational descriptors in describing their relationship with Christ. Knowing Christ is relational because He is a person.

Jesus did not ask this man about the first four commandments that deal with internal works of genuine relationship to God—no other gods before Him, no idols, not taking His name in vain, and remembering the Sabbath. This was for good reason. These laws were kept more internally rather than externally. No one but you and God can know if you are really worshipping another God. Only you and God can know if you have changed Him into something else—an idol. It is entirely possible to worship the right God the wrong way and create an idol; thus, it is not the same God. Only you and God can know if you take His name in vain. Taking God's name in vain means to lift it up to nothingness. Only you and God can know if you are making corporate worship and the meeting with other believers a priority.

Do you catch the drift here? We can totally look one way outwardly—pious, good, religious—and actually not have a relationship with God. Ephesians 2:8 says, "For by grace you have been saved through faith. And this is not your own doing; it is the gift of God." A gift by definition can't be earned; it is something given us that we could not attain on our own. Salvation, a relationship with God, is difficult for many to comprehend because we are good present givers and not gift receivers.

Just like you, I give some people presents at Christmastime. Now, let's face it, we are obligated to give some people presents every year. And whether we say this or not, we have different price points for our various relational groupings. So your family probably gets more per person for presents. Then maybe some close friends get a little less than your family. As other people get farther out on your relational concentric circles, they get less and less to the point that some people just get a "Merry Christmas" fist bump. You get the idea. Now over time some people figure this out as well. So, while it is never said, I have some $50 relationships, some $25 relationships, some gift card relationships, and so on. I know this is true because they give me about what I give them every year. This is not really gift giving. This is present exchanging. We would probably just do better keeping our money and doing the fist-bump thing. That being said, we don't really understand gift giving. Only God gives you a relationship with Himself; you can't earn it.

A word of warning—we are not saved by our works. It's a gift. But we are saved to work. Are you tracking? We can never earn a relationship with God. If you have a relationship with Him, that is all on Him. But, since you have a relationship with Him, it will be evidenced by your works (James 2:17). Works are not the reason for salvation but the result of salvation. Therefore, we cannot be lazy disciples. We will work for His glory as a result of the relationship we have with Him.

Do you have a relationship with God, or are you caught in the trap of religion like this rich, young man? Here is the reality: if you have a relationship with Jesus, you know it. I have a relationship with my wife, and there is no way you could convince me we are not married. I know I have a relationship with her because there was a day, nearly twenty years ago, when we went into a church and we were not married. Once we got in the church, we said some vows in front of our family and friends, we gave each other some rings and kissed, and the preacher introduced us as husband and wife. We went into the church not married, and we came out married. In the years that have passed, I have further proof that we are married—a home loan, income tax statements, pictures, and children. I could keep going on, but you get the point. If God has allowed us to be certain about temporal relationships, like marriage, doesn't it make sense that He would want us to be more certain about an eternal relationship with Him?

The Barrier of Riches

But the story goes on. Jesus tells the religiously sincere man, "'One thing you still lack. Sell all that you have and distribute to the poor, and you will have treasure in heaven; and come, follow me.'

But when he heard these things, he became very sad, for he was extremely rich" (Luke 18:22–23).

Jesus quickly cuts to the heart of this man's life. While everything looked OK on the outside and while everyone saw a devoutly religious man, Jesus knew what was going on with this young religious man, and He knows what is going on with you. There is a real danger in respecting Jesus as a Teacher and not acknowledging Him as Lord. Jesus is the glory of God incarnate. He is mighty in all His ways. One day every knee will bow and tongue confess that Jesus Christ is Lord, to the glory of God the Father (Phil. 2:10). This man respected Jesus, but he did not give Jesus the glory due Him.

In the fall of 1996, I was a freshman at Baylor University and training to become an intramural referee. Apparently God felt I needed to learn some humility, and the dog-cussing I would receive from little Baptist debutantes who were rooting for their boyfriends when I missed a call was the cure.

One day, while waiting for my training to begin, I noticed a group of guys stretching. Being above average in intelligence and under average in height, I deduced that these were members of the Baylor track team. Not meeting too many strangers, I began to introduce myself to these student athletes when I noticed this one athlete was wearing an unusual pair of gold Nike track shoes. I commented on how cool the shoes were and asked the gentleman if he was a member of the track team. He grinned and said that he used to be. Immediately the other track members began to laugh among themselves. I went on and asked him what he did for a living. After all, I was just starting off my college career. I wanted to know what to expect. He informed me that he ran track for a living. Taken aback by his response, I asked him if a person could make a good living as a professional runner. He subtly said that it had worked out for him. At this point his fellow athletes have all but fallen down laughing. I just figured someone said something funny—not thinking it was me.

The group ran off about the time my supervisor walked up. My supervisor said, "Did you just meet Michael Johnson?" I said, "I guess. Was he one of the guys I was just talking to?" He went on to inform me that the man with the gold shoes was at that time the fastest man in the world. Weeks before Michael Johnson had won gold medals in both the two-hundred-meter and four-hundred-meter sprints in the Atlanta Olympics. At the time I talked to him, his face was on the Wheaties box. You can be in the presence of greatness and be completely clueless. I know I was.

This young man did not know who Jesus was and what He demanded. Lords rule over people. They have authority to tell people what to do and what not to do. Jesus tells this young man to sell all of his riches and give the proceeds to the poor. Now, it is important to remember, riches are not bad, in and of themselves; they are neutral. But, when riches become a god, the idol must be killed. The love of money is the root of all kinds of evil (1 Tim. 6:10), and one cannot serve God and money (Matt. 6:24). When Jesus is your Lord, you realize you may own many things, but you possess nothing. Everything is to be used at His direction.

People in Jesus' day believed material blessing was a sign of spiritual favor from God. While we, in our day, might not make this same claim, it is implied. We naturally assume material blessings are a result of spiritual blessings. In the Old Testament it is obvious that God blessed men like Abraham, David, and Solomon materially for their personal obedience and to let other nations see the tangible results of their obedience. The Old Testament is marked by the accumulation of wealth. By the time we get to the New Testament, we see that the liquidating of materials goods represents the obedience of early church followers. Throughout the book of Acts, we see believers giving to meet others' needs. We live in the tension of both of these realities.

     While Jesus might never ask you or me to completely liquate everything and give it to Him, He has the right and the ability to ask that of us. Jesus will have us destroy any idol that emerges in our life. I imagine this young, rich ruler was outwardly generous to people. Jews in that day had an obligation to take care of the poor. Religious Jews would regularly give out alms to the poor, like this young man most likely did. Now Jesus was instructing this young man to give not just generously but sacrificially. Jesus wanted this man to give it all away. When you love Jesus as Lord, you love who and what He loves. From the beginning of Christ's ministry until now, Jesus identified with and served the poor. This man didn't have Jesus as his Lord because he didn't share Jesus' heart. He didn't love the poor. This man probably thought the investment in the poor was senseless and extravagant.

     One of my favorite people in world is a man named Richard Galloway, the former president of New York Relief Ministry in New York City. For over twenty-five years New York Relief has served the homeless population of New York by connecting them to Christian social service agencies and meeting immediate physical needs through feeding buses throughout the city. One day I was in Richard's office, which was plastered with large, black-and-white photos of homeless people that New York Relief had ministered to over the years. Galloway gazed around that office, stared at each face, and said, "Kris, Jesus shows up in some pretty freaky-looking dudes!" In that moment I was reminded of Jesus' words about the poor: "Truly, I say to you, as you did it to one of the least of these my brothers, you did it to me" (Matt. 25:45). Galloway went on to say, "The poor are not a problem to be solved but a portal to God's heart."

Jesus valued poor people for many reasons but, I suspect, mostly because He was one. We worship a homeless man. Poor people are served by rich people because they need the provision of the rich. But rich people need poor people to teach them lessons about faith. But for rich men then and now, one indicator that Jesus is Lord is demonstrated if we share His heart for His people. The rich man in this story did not value what Jesus valued.

From time to time I have people ask me why we as a church go to other places, cities, and countries and not take all of the time, money, and resources and focus it all locally. The answer is simple—Jesus's heart is bigger than just where we live. God's love is bigger than just where you live. John 3:16 says, "For God so loved the world." God's love is not for only select parts of the world. It is easy to love our own part of the world and hard to love the entire world. We like our part of the world, and other parts of the world smell, look, and act differently from our part of the world. But, when Jesus is your Lord, you love what and whom He loves—and it is ever expanding.

Here is the tragedy of the story. Jesus, seeing that the young man had become sad, said, "How difficult it is for those who have wealth to enter the kingdom of God! For it is easier for a camel to go through the eye of a needle than for a rich person to enter the kingdom of God" (Luke 18:24–25).

This man chose his riches over Christ. He wanted to keep his religion, which placated his ambition, tempered his guilt, and helped him justify his riches. Many people in our time do the same thing. Riches are so dangerous because they make people self-sufficient, self-confident, and self-centered. Rich people make decisions based on comfort, ease, and luxury. Jesus said, "How difficult it is for those who have wealth to enter the kingdom of heaven." It is hard for rich people to go to heaven. Rich people perceive they do not need God; they have no needs.

Recently our church acquired a new church property. This was nothing short of the hand of God working in two churches, both over one hundred years old, to bring about His great glory. The two locations are eleven miles apart. In studying the demographics of the new area, I discovered the average home price is over five hundred thousand dollars. What I find more intriguing is the number of young families who live in this area. It is nothing to see some incredible home, with a BMW and a Range Rover in the driveway, with Little Tikes play equipment in the yard. Not surprising, the overwhelming majority of the city does not attend a church anywhere. Why? Rich people do not need God.

Annually we take our faith family on mission trips around the world. We go to industrialized nations and developing nations with the gospel. Every year we find many more people are willing to give their lives to Christ in developing nations than in industrialized nations. The answer is simple—rich people do not need God. And remember, most of you reading this book are rich—you are loaded. It is harder for you to make heaven because of your affluence.

But here is the good news. While it is difficult, it is not impossible. With God all things are possible. Check it out: "Those who heard it said, 'Then who can be saved?' But he said, 'What is impossible with man is possible with God.' And Peter said, 'See, we have left our homes and followed you.' And he said to them, 'Truly, I say to you, there is no one who has left house or wife or brothers or parents or children, for the sake of the kingdom of God, who will not receive many times more in this time, and in the age to come eternal life'" (Luke 18:26–30).

God can reach rich people. It is not impossible for Him. He can help the rich use their affluence for His influence. Only God can break dependency on the self. And the best part is, God can help rich people trade in their earthly trinkets for eternal treasure that will not perish.

A Decision

I believe this story of the rich young ruler is the scariest story in the Bible. Think about it: this man left the presence of Jesus convicted, not converted. He knew his real god was his possessions, not Jesus. The man left condemned. He knew what his future held. Do you? People can't reject Christ as Lord, not have Christ's heart for the lost world, and one day die and expect to go to heaven because they did some good things. This rich man died and went to hell. You might say, "You don't know that." The text gives us no indication that the man ever repented of his sin and turned to Christ as his Lord. People who reject Christ go to hell.

Here is the kicker: I imagine this man went back to leading at his synagogue. I bet, after this encounter with Christ, he did not lose one bit of standing with the other well-adjusted religious types he associated with in his town. I imagine he still made significant donations to religious work. I am almost certain he gave money to the poor. He might have even doubled his giving effort. He probably prayed in some superficial way. He might have even memorized some pithy little religious sayings. But one day he died. He breathed his last. And he went to hell.

And you know what the people did who were left, like his family and religious friends? They had a nice service. They sang some songs. They talked about all the "good things" he did, and maybe that made them feel better. But it did not change his eternal destination. Religion and riches won out over Christ and chasing the awesome glory of God.

Questions

1. You are chasing someone. Who is it?
2. Does your heart love the people and things Christ loves?
3. What will people say about you at your funeral?

Endnotes

[1] John Piper, Brothers, We Are Not Professionals: A Plea to Pastors for a Radical Ministry (Nashville: Broadman & Holman, 2002), 6–7.

[2] K. P. Yohannan, *Touching Godliness* (Carrollton: GFA Books, 2008), 176.

[3] Mark Sayers, *The Road Trip that Changed the World* (Chicago: Moody Publishers, 2012), 176.

[4] Jonathan Sacks, Covenant and Conversation: Genesis: The Book of Beginnings (Jerusalem: Maggid, 2009).

[5] "Angelina Jolie," accessed October 23, 2014, http://www.celebatheists.com/wiki/Angelina_Jolie.

[6] Mack Stiles, *Mark of the Messenger* (Downers Grove: Intervarsity Press, 2010), 39–42.

[7] Audrey Barrick, "Survey: Most Young People Are 'Lost' Despite 'Christian' Label," *The Christian Post*, accessed October 23, 2014, http://www.christianpost.com/news/survey-most-young-people-are-lost-despite-christian-label-44931.

[8] "The Yi Ethnic Minority," accessed October 23, 2014, http://www.china.org.cn/e-groups/shaoshu/shao-2-yi.htm.

[9] Dietrich Bonhoeffer, *The Cost of Discipleship* (New York: Simon and Schuster, 1995), 64.

[10] Ibid., 89.

[11] Ibid., 43–47.

[12] Eric Mataxas, *Bonhoeffer: Pastor, Martyr, Prophet, Spy* (Dallas: Thomas Nelson, 2010), 531–33.

[13] Eberhard Bethge, *Dietrich Bonhoeffer: A Biography* (Minneapolis: Fortress, 2000), 927.

[14] Alexander McConnell, William Revell Moody, Arthur Percy Fitt, *Record of Christian Work*, Vol. 25 (New York: Record of Christian Work Company, 1906), 47.

[15] A. W. Tozer, *The Pursuit of God* (Camp Hill: Christian Publications, 1982), 45.

[16] Alex and Brett Harris, *Do Hard Things* (Colorado Springs: Multnomah Books, 2008), 31–33.

[17] Tozer, *The Pursuit of God*, 19.

[18] "Black and Blue Lagoon of Buxton," accessed October 24, 2014, http://www.atlasobscura.com/places/blue-lagoon-of-buxton.

Made in the USA
San Bernardino, CA
09 March 2015